# DIAMOND

## THE MEMOIR OF A LOST DAUGHTER OF JAPAN

ETSUKO DIAMOND MIYAGI

Cataloging-in-Publication Data is on file with the Library of Congress.

ISBN 979-8-9908299-0-9 (eBook)
ISBN 979-8-9908299-1-6 (Paperback)
ISBN 979-8-9908299-2-3 (Hardback)

PRINTED IN THE UNITED STATES OF AMERICA

*To the Miyagi Family–*
*Hideshin, Teruko, and Tomoko–*
*we will cherish your dedication and sacrifice*
*in our hearts and minds forever.*

*To the people of Oshiro Village,*
*Kitanakagusuku-son, Nakagami-gun,*
*Okinawa Prefecture, Japan,*
*for welcoming us with open arms*
*into your community,*
*our gratitude knows no bounds.*

# CONTENTS

CHAPTER ONE

# CURSED RAIN

My father was a Japanese businessman from Okinawa who owned an abaca plantation in Mindanao in the Philippines. With a Japanese war on the horizon, my parents took me and my baby sister away to the mountainside near Davao City. My parents had been warned that it wasn't safe for us there either, but what choice did they have? Their only hope was to find refuge in the remote village deep within those hills, which hadn't yet been affected by this conflict between Japan and its neighbors.

I was six years old.

I know this now because I have been told. Perhaps I would have kept many early childhood memories if my life had been safe and ordinary. But my life was split in half by a violent tragedy, which rendered everything that had come before—my first six years in the world—into fragments I could barely gather.

Forever after, I remembered my parents, my Japanese family, only in dreams. In those dreams, I could almost recollect the faces from another life as they spoke to me in a language I had forgotten.

"Otousan," I would call my father. "Okaasan," I would call my mother. The other words were gone, and those two names would soon fade.

Sometimes in my dreams, I saw myself in Japan at the low table with others, where we had dinner. There were fleeting visions of Okaasan lovingly scolding me when I was naughty or Otousan seated on the floor beside my bed as I went to sleep. Other young faces smiled and spoke to me playfully, but their features receded into the dimness, and I did not know if they had ever been real. I remembered feeling a hand in mine, a clapping game, and the smell of cherries. But just as I reached toward these dream people, just as I almost understood their words, they slipped away.

For a time in those dreams, I felt happy and loved, as if transported to a brief fairytale that happened to another child. But in my waking life, I had almost no memories from before the awful day I hid under the bamboo floorboards of a hut in the jungle.

While I slept fitfully, huddled in a ball, sweat breaking over me, the dream always turned into a nightmare. Some details never changed, and others were slippery enough that remembering precisely what had happened was impossible. I dreamed I was outside under the hot sun, and the sky above was filled with roaring airplanes. I did not understand what that meant, not at the time, and I crawled under the bamboo house to play.

Why was I outdoors under a warring sky? Okaasan had ordered me outside to keep me out of the way as she and Otousan rushed around the house in a dreadful panic. Otousan searched for essential papers, and Okaasan strapped the baby to her back. Wait...the baby...had there been a baby? I thought I remembered hearing the wails of an infant, but there was so much cacophonous noise that day. Were they only the shrill cries of the jungle birds? The dream was ever elusive; sometimes, the objects shifted. I would rather imagine the shrieks of wild animals than think that once I'd had a tiny baby sister who vanished forever from my life.

Frantically Okaasan gathered food for another trip that we must take immediately. Otousan helped her with a heavy case, but it fell to the floor, crashing open, its contents rolling out of reach. I hear their footsteps padding quickly from one side of the hut to the other. They both rush about, clumsy and afraid, snapping back and forth at each other. The dimensions of the dream house change, and my parents cannot find the doorway. Time is running out. They look between the floorboards to try to find me. Frightened, I listen from beneath the floor, drawing symbols in the dirt with a stick. I dream that the characters have hieroglyphic meanings, which could save us if only I could read them. I cannot.

In the dream, I hear three men enter our house. They are stealing from us, turning over furniture, kicking it angrily aside as they smash through boxes and drawers. They have enormous knives in their hands, which they brandish at my parents. I watch in horror through the bamboo as Otousan argues with them, as Okaasan weeps and pleads, her hands up before her, and the baby wails in fear. The wails transform into the cries of terrified jungle animals. I clap my hands over my ears.

This part is the most difficult, yet it is the part I can never forget. I wish this awful episode in my life would fade as everything else had instead of coming back time and again with such terrible, red clarity. But fresh in my mind, this part remains: The men swing their machetes and do something that I, as a child, did not know was possible. Otousan and Okaasan's heads fall from their bodies. Okaasan's head rolls like a heavy ball over the place where I hide, and I scream, high and loud.

That scream wakes me, too late to spare me from seeing.

Maybe I struggled and scrambled to escape when the killers came under the house to get me. Perhaps I sat dumbfounded, unable to believe what was happening. Did my parents' blood drip through the bamboo like a cursed rain? Did it stain me? Did I hear my baby sister one last time? Did I even see what became of her? Oh mercy, did she ever even exist—or was she just another version of me, a little girl in the middle of a massacre? Did I scream again, did I cry or whimper, or was I silent while the Bagobo men took me away? I don't know.

I don't know. The dream ends, and everything I want so badly to remember fades.

Rather than waking with a start or a cry, I always

awakened slowly, wrenching my way out from under the tendrils of that dreadful, confused memory. My trembling continued as I rose from a cardboard mat on the ground, to face the daily life that was now mine: a Japanese child in a Bagobo village on the Philippine island of Mindanao.

At first, the Bagobo men took me to a decrepit nipa hut in the middle of nowhere. Shocked and speechless, I stared around at the alien place. The walls were made of leaves. There were no beds or furniture, no appliances. A small fire pit in the center of the room served as the place for cooking. At night, the people there slept on the hard ground, with cardboard and leaves for bedding.

I was miserable, and itchy, lying surrounded by half a dozen people as they snored and muttered in their sleep. I sweated and cried as mosquitos landed on me, their burring wings loud in my ears. I was always hungry, and food was scarce. The men hunted and brought back dead animals; the women dug roots from the ground. It was never enough to feed us all, and I was usually the last one to eat. Each day was an eternity. I could not make sense of what was happening.

For a long time, I waited for my parents to come and find me. Each noise I heard, each unfamiliar sound, made my head snap up in hope—finally, they had come to take me home. I don't know when I stopped looking up. The hope faded, as their faces faded, as the Japanese language disappeared into the far corners of my memory.

Had any of the things in my nightmares ever really happened? At least some of it had to be true; otherwise, why was I there? Because the fact was, I did not belong there, and I was seldom allowed to forget that.

The people of Magpet called me "Bata," which means "child." The families fought over who got to keep me, a Japanese trophy snatched from their attackers. I was traded from house to house—a commodity with value that I did not want. They gave me endless chores and made me work hard, as a sign of their victory over a country I could not remember. I never went to school. I never fit in, for I was never meant to or allowed to fit in.

I could count from one to ten in Japanese, *ichi, ni, san*... aside from my own face, this was my sole scrap of evidence, that once I had spoken another language, and that I was from another place.

CHAPTER TWO

# A CHILD IN MAGPET

When I was about ten in 1948, I was finally adopted into a kinder family. Though they were penniless, they at least saw that I was fed and treated me more gently; they didn't strike me or punish me for mistakes. I was relieved to be under their care.

Yet nothing ever felt certain. I might be bartered or snatched away at any moment. The fight to own me reached a pitch of jealousy that threatened to disrupt the village.

I never knew who, but someone reported to the Bagobo Chief, Doming Apostol, that a Japanese child was being handed around the tribe. His duty was to resolve the dispute, as he controlled the town and surrounding farms and villages. Doming ordered that I be brought to his home. He looked me over and spoke to the man acting as my guardian. I was frightened to be the subject of such scrutiny and kept my head ducked, my eyes lowered. I had never been inside so fine a house before. Standing in the middle of the Chief's grand front hall, I felt small and dirty. Distantly on the upper floor of the house, I heard children's laughter.

"Where did this child come from?" the Chief asked my adopted guardian. "How is it that a Japon girl is being traded around like a goat from hut to hut?"

My adopted guardian told the story as best he could, but even he really did not know the full truth. The circumstances of my life were already a matter of guesswork and rumor.

"She is a good girl, quiet, a hard worker," my adopted guardian told Doming. "The other children in Magpet torment her because she is different—the adults sometimes aren't much better. And our neighbors want to take her from us because they want the extra hands to work. My wife and I have come to like little Bata, however. Our own children are mostly grown. It is pleasant to have a youngster again. We will keep her, with your approval, Chief."

Doming agreed, but said, "I won't have this child being a matter of in-fighting and jealousy throughout my district. She's hardly older than my own daughter, and if I thought Erlinda was being bartered around or bullied, I'd not stand for it. Children shouldn't live in terror. If the trouble continues, we'll have to do something."

My guardian took this to heart as we returned to their humble hut. For a time things seemed to improve. Doming's word spread around the village: no more fighting over little Japon Bata. It didn't stop the children from chasing or badgering me incessantly, but that was easier to endure as long as I had a relatively secure place to sleep at night.

It wasn't uncommon in the Bagobo tribe for older men to seek out younger brides, regardless of what relationship they may have had. Girls might be wedded off when they were only eleven or twelve years old, to men who gave their families money or livestock in exchange. Sometimes the tribal leaders were simply able to take whatever, or whomever, they wanted. Having very young brides was still considered a matter of pride and status.

I was hardly more than ten when Datu, a man of almost forty years, took notice of my potential as his wife-to-be. Whenever I encountered him in the village, his gaze made my skin crawl. I felt an icy chill run through me each time he sized me up with that calculating look. His presence filled the room with an overwhelming stench; it clung to him like a second skin. He clearly spent more time eating than doing anything else. His teeth were stained yellow from constantly chewing tobacco, and when he spat out the juice, it hardly ever landed in an appropriate place. The thought of being married to this man was a whole new nightmare for me.

My guardian did not take kindly to Datu's proposal, engaging in heated arguments with the man on several occasions to protect me. "She's much too young," my adopted father insisted. "I'm not selling a child into marriage; you're old enough to be her granddad."

"She's not even your child," replied my would-be suitor. "What difference does it make to you? She's another mouth to feed. I have a large farm, plenty of work to keep her busy, plenty of food to go around."

"It's impossible," said my adopted father. "I wouldn't allow it for my own daughters, and I won't allow it for Bata. It's an old-fashioned, brutal practice. Doming doesn't approve of it, either."

"The Chief!" remarked Datu scornfully. "What does he care? She's not even Filipino. You should take my offer now. It's a better price than you'd get from anyone else." He did indeed have a farm outside Magpet; he had brought a wagon holding a couple of bags of corn and a cage of clucking chickens. It was troubling to hear my value put in those terms. But my adopted father refused again.

"Soon you won't have any choice," said Datu threateningly. "There are ways to make her my wife without your permission."

"You leave the child alone," replied my guardian with equal vehemence. Datu stalked away, taking his corn and chickens with him, and I prayed that was the end of it.

But it was not. One day I was sent on an errand to retrieve drinking water from a spring well about two miles away from home. I found myself alone—something that did not often happen. I was never completely at ease with being around others, seldom knowing what kind of treatment to expect. Time alone gave me a mixed feeling of freedom and apprehension, of safety and concern. The world had already taught me that terrible things could happen instantly.

As I briskly walked toward the stream with my pots, I became certain that someone was following me. Years of dodging blows from bullying children had made me extremely sensitive to my surroundings, and now my nerves prickled, telling me that someone was nearby, close behind, hiding. I walked faster. Running would make them chase me, I knew, so I strode along quickly—so fast my pots rattled and thumped against each other. If I could just make it to the stream, there would be other people there, and I could only hope they might protect me.

Suddenly, in a secluded glen along the pathway, a man stepped from the jungle directly in front of me. It was Datu. He looked winded, but determined, and the smile he gave me was not friendly or kind. "Your papa sent me to get you," he said. "You're to come with me now."

I shook my head, backing away. I was too afraid to speak.

"Don't be difficult," Datu warned, stepping toward me. He moved faster than I thought he would, and tried to grab my arm. I squealed in fear and yanked back. "You'll be in big trouble if you disobey—your papa will beat you, and I will too. Come with me at once!"

The same careful observation I'd learned for self-preservation had also given me a sharp awareness of dishonesty. I didn't see it often; most of the people I knew had few reasons to lie. But Datu was lying to me now. My adopted papa hadn't traded me away, and Datu was trying to steal me. I didn't understand how or why this should be the case, but I knew that he could do something to me that would force the marriage. He had threatened as much to my adopted guardians.

When I wouldn't stand still or cooperate, Datu's face grew enraged. "When you live under my roof, you'll learn to obey me, or—"

As he spoke, he lunged, his huge spread of arms like the wings of a terrifying bird swooping toward me. I screamed again and hurled my water pots at him. They struck well. One hit his hand, but the other landed squarely in the middle of his body, and I knew that the boys in the village always joked about how much it hurt to be hit there. Datu whoofed and doubled over, saying terrible words.

I didn't waste a second, but tore away from him, racing back down the path toward town. I was small, and I had learned to be quick. I hoped he would be unable to catch me. Unless he had brought help! In terror, I searched the jungle for emerging faces as my feet pounded down the path. I heard Datu behind me, shouting, and not nearly as far away as I would have hoped. He was slower than I, but his legs were much longer, and anger drove his speed.

My breath was rough and wheezing by the time I burst back into Magpet, with Datu still thrashing through the jungle behind me. I glanced around. My adopted parents would not be at the hut now—they were working outside of the village today. I could not trust that any other village people would listen to me. Datu had influence with the tribe. I did not know where I could hide.

I made a choice at that moment which would forever change my destiny. I remembered the house of Chief Doming. He had frightened me, but my adopted papa trusted his wisdom. And the Chief had a daughter near my age. I hoped to find help there.

I darted toward the center of Magpet, toward the Chief's fine home. There were workers all around the yard, and as

I scrambled by them, they shouted at me. "Where do you think you're going? You can't just come running up here!"

One of them asked, "Isn't she that Japon orphan?"

Datu was at the yard just as I reached the house's front door. "Stop that girl!" he shouted to the men. "She's in a lot of trouble!"

Some of the men looked like they might move toward me. I pounded at the door, scrabbled at its latch. The door gave way, and I tumbled into the front hall of the Apostol house, sobbing.

Several feet away from me I saw the most beautiful woman I had ever beheld—tall and regal, in silky clothes that looked softer than feathers. She regarded me with surprise, then looked at the men outside. I did not know it at the time, but yard workers were not permitted inside the front hall. They were too dirty.

Datu stepped into the room. "Lady Adela, my apologies," he panted with extreme deference. "This girl ran from me to escape punishment. I'll collect her and be gone in a moment."

It was against my nature to speak out for myself; in fact, I seldom spoke more than a few short words at a time. Today, though, I had to do something. I had nothing to lose.

"Please may I speak to Chief Doming?" I gasped, trembling all over. "He knows my papa. Datu wants to make me get married, and papa says I don't have to."

The woman called Lady Adela cocked an eyebrow at Datu. "Isn't this child a bit young for marriage?"

"She's the Japon orphan," Datu explained. "Better she has a husband than continue to be a burden on the village."

"Well, I can't have this ruckus in my hall," replied Lady Adela. "Datu, please wait outside while we find Doming. No, leave the child to us for now. Little girl, you may go wait in the kitchen." She turned slightly aside to speak to a maid who had appeared to see what the fuss was about. "Take this girl to the kitchen and get her washed up before she touches something—she's filthy."

With the maid's assistance, I was cleaned up, given a drink of water, and told to go wait in the backyard. There I observed an enormous stretch of land covered with beautiful fruit trees. As I calmed down, I took in everything about this magical place. The maid who had brusquely helped me wash my hands and face had gotten water from a pipe *inside* the house. I had never seen such a thing.

Sometimes faces came to the grand house's windows to peer down at me outside. I waited with my knees hugged to my chest, sick to my stomach at the thought of being forced to marry Datu.

It was a long time before my adopted papa finally came to speak to me.

"Well, you've had a busy day," he said. He wasn't angry, as I had feared he might be. Instead, he looked rather sad. "Old Datu says you threw your pots at him and injured him. Is that right?"

He chuckled softly when I didn't answer. Then he said, "Bata, we think you might be safer if you stayed here. Chief Doming has offered you a job in his home, and you would have a place to sleep here. It's not that we want to give you away. You understand, though, that we cannot protect you from the likes of Datu. If you come to work for Chief Doming, Datu—and everyone else—will have to leave you alone."

The thought of changing homes again made me sad, but my fear of Datu was worse. Deep inside me, a steely little core of strength was glad I had thrown the pots at Datu, glad I had hurt him. If I hadn't saved myself, I couldn't imagine what might have happened.

Still, because I liked my adopted papa, I apologized quietly for the trouble I had caused.

"This is not your fault," he said. "And we will still be in the village; you will see us all the time, right down the road. It's a fine idea. Now, come and thank the Chief for his graciousness."

As far as I knew, I had no name other than Bata. Rumors around town said that Chief Doming had jewels hidden away somewhere, but who knows if this is true? I heard the story told that way because Chief Doming Apostol informed me, "From now on, your name is Diamond. Here in my home, you will be safe."

## CHAPTER THREE

# A HOUSE OF IMPORTANCE

I had never imagined such a house as the one in which the Apostol family lived, and its wonders continued to amaze me for some time after I became one of the staff. Located in the center of Magpet town, most of which the Apostol family owned, it was the largest residence I had ever seen. Before I was brought inside the grounds, I had only glimpsed it from between the trees outside, or heard whispers of the important things that happened there.

An enormous hall occupied the ground floor, used for council meetings and parties. There were two kitchens and a dining room, and a spare room to store produce and vegetables harvested from the property or from Chief Doming's many tenant farms. Upstairs were six bedrooms and a large parlor where the Apostol family lived and gathered; it was their private family space away from the bustle of the ground floor.

The sheer luxury of the home astounded me. This was the first house I had ever known to have kerosene lamps. There was running water, as Chief Doming had a water well and a huge tank for water at the back of the house. For the years I had lived with the Bagobos, I was sent to fetch water from the river. Fetching water was a child's job, and I was the lowest of the children. Each week I crossed difficult, hilly, and jungle terrains while carrying buckets and pots of water that were almost as heavy as I was. The fact that water was here on the property seemed like a miracle.

Simply to have a clean, comfortable place to sleep was such a relief. I was put to work at once in this important house, and expected to do as much as any adult. I worked alongside a dozen other servants in the home's two kitchens, because food was plentiful and meals were always in demand. The house seldom ran out of visitors. Each month, Chief Doming held tribal meetings. When the Bagobo people came, they came by the hundreds, and they all had to be fed. When I saw Datu at such meetings, I avoided him; I was crafty at remaining unseen. If ordered to bring him a drink or food, I did so without meeting his eyes, and pretended like I didn't know who he was. How he glared at me! But he never dared say a word.

Chief Doming's property was covered in bountiful fruit trees, over fifty types. In addition to rice farms, he also owned a goose farm, so that there was never a shortage of eggs or meat. We cooked and served huge meals, then cleaned up, only to cook and serve again, a constant parade of dishes delivered to the dining room in the back wing of the house.

As the Apostol family and their guests ate together, the servants stood aside, ensuring that everything the family desired was on the table. Only when they finished and retired from the room, did we get to quickly sit and eat, so that the clearing and cleaning up could begin. Despite that rushing, we were fed well, and it was a blessing to no longer suffer from hunger.

The Apostol house had one terrifying aspect for me: a yawning expanse of basement that no one wanted to enter. The huge room was created before World War II, and extended beneath the entire length of the ground floor. It was surprisingly deep, twenty-five feet from floor to ceiling. The room was installed as a sort of bunker, a hiding place for ammunition, food, and medicine, and could have served as a hiding place during the war. The staff gossiped that Chief Doming kept treasures down there, which were guarded by the enormous snakes that slithered across the floor.

Thankfully, my chores never required me to go down there. I dared once to venture inside the basement door, just to see what had the maids so frightened. My childish imagination filled the cavernous space with enigmatic sounds and monstrous creatures, and I hurried out.

I was treated as something of an oddity, and because I was different, the cooks and the housekeepers were quick to scold me for my mistakes. It was easy for them to take their irritations out on me. Servants of higher class worked inside the house, and servants of lower class did the outside work—gardening, harvesting, and caring for the grounds. I had no class, no status, and no one to stand up for me. I was the symbol of a conquered enemy. I had to obey everyone, do whatever I was told to do.

Chief Doming had named me "Diamond," but the staff always clipped the final "d" sound from the name when they spoke to me.

"Diamon, you stupid little fool," they might bite at me, if I dropped a plate or forgot a chore. Or they might warn me, "If you want to earn your place in the Apostol household, you'll have to do better than that, Diamon." I heard in their tones that they assumed my "foreignness" made me slow, though to my mind I knew no other country except this one. The meaner servants sometimes called me the "stupid Japon girl" if they were in a bad mood or I got something wrong.

Never mind that. Long ago, I'd grown accustomed to being called names. I learned to move fast and anticipate everyone's wishes, so they'd have no reason to snap at me or insult me. You see, what those dismissive servants did not know was that this: a sprawling household of wealth I could not comprehend, was the first place where I felt truly safe. Out in the village, even under the protection of my kinder guardians, I was bullied and harassed. I never knew what might come next, who would be my next master, who would be the next one to shout at me or strike me. In the village, I'd grown adept at being small, hiding in plain sight, drawing as little attention as possible.

Suddenly in the Apostol home, I found myself for the first time in a situation where things were predictable. I had a real bed to sleep in instead of straw on the ground. I was fed. There was a stability here that children need. And I was still in most ways a child, though my eyes had seen things that had aged my soul, even if my waking mind could barely remember.

The other servants were mostly too busy to be overtly cruel to me, and once I showed myself to be a reliable helper, things generally went smoothly. I wanted to remain there and worked extremely hard to ensure that they would keep me.

Aside from helping with the constant need of feeding the house's family and countless guests, I cleaned the house and yard, and helped with the laundry. But my favorite duty was to look after the little Apostol children.

The Apostols had five children when I arrived, and more came in the years that followed. The eldest, Erlinda, was eight, only a couple of years younger than I.

Erlinda astonished me as much as her opulent home. She was a determined, stubborn, and spoiled girl. She was as distant as a princess, like her mother—yet, like her father, forceful and commanding.

Erlinda had nothing to do with me. I was there to work and earn my keep, not to befriend Chief Doming's eldest daughter. But I watched her from the corner of my eye, the way one might watch a mythical animal: this girl whose parents doted on her, who had everything she wanted, who went to school and knew how to read and write, who was praised for her intelligence and admired for her status. I do not think it was envy, but fascination, which made me gaze at her when she wasn't looking. I dared sometimes to wonder what it might be like, to be such a little girl.

After Erlinda came Dodong, who was six, and Orlando, only four. Rodolfo and Rachel were the babies. I often looked after them as they tumbled around in the orchards. I helped feed them and cleaned up after them, too. I loved minding the children, because they were too young to know that I was different or undeserving. They adored me in the way that children will adore anyone who is kind and caring to them.

Sometimes when I played with them under the shade of the fruit trees, I felt like they were my own little family. It was the first time I could remember feeling this kind of love, and feeling I was needed, except in my dreams. In the years that followed, two more daughters arrived, Evelyn in 1952, and Sarah in 1954.

So no, I had no desire to leave the Apostol household. Things were better for me there than they had ever been before. Chief Doming barely interacted with me after that first day; he was a very busy man with children of his own, but I was grateful to him, nonetheless.

Though I was uneducated, out of necessity I was a clever child who knew how to listen, how to read the moods of the people around me, and how to keep myself as safe as I could manage. I grabbed at knowledge the way little Rodolfo and Rachel grabbed mangos from the trees in the yard. As time passed, I kept my ears open to learn what I could, and heard the stories of how this ruling household of the Bagobo had come to be.

CHAPTER FOUR

# CHIEF DOMING AND LADY ADELA

The servants gossiped, never to me, but always around me, as if I were too stupid to understand them. As I scrubbed laundry up and down a washboard in the yard, up to my elbows in soap and water, I could hear through the windows as the maids chattered inside. One had been here long enough to have heard the story; the other was new enough to still be enamored with this powerful family. The older maid told the younger that Chief Doming had come to Mindanao from the northern city of Cebu, to escape the angry father of a woman he'd gotten "in trouble."

"The girl's father was going to murder him!" she confided as they swept and dusted the main hall. "The threats on his life are why he came all the way south."

Through the window, I spied the wide-eyed younger maid, as she leaned hopefully into a tale of star-crossed love. "Was he too low-class for her?" Was she too low-class for *him?*"

"No, it wasn't that—they were the same class. The problem was, they were third cousins."

"Oh my! But—"

"Their love was strictly forbidden," affirmed the first maid. "Their families would not permit it. Her name was Inday."

"And were they deeply, madly in love with each other?"

The first maid looked at her younger companion with sympathy, as if this girl must be quite unworldly. "Of course they were. They were young. He was handsome, and she was beautiful, and they were probably soulmates. Otherwise, how do you think she got in trouble? Well, of course they met in secret, you know. Until it was too late, and everyone found out. And Doming had to flee the wrath of Inday's father!"

"It sounds like a movie," the younger maid said wistfully. "Whatever happened to her and the child?"

Her companion had to admit the limits to her own knowledge, and speculated, "The love of her life was gone forever, and poor Inday was left alone to raise their illegitimate son. She must have flung herself from a bridge in despair. Wouldn't you?"

Her morbid guess was wrong, but I would not learn that until many years later.

"Then the child must be an orphan!" lamented the younger maid. "Rejected by his family...his mother a suicide... what a tragedy!"

"I imagine someday there will have to be vengeance done," agreed the older. She relished the idea.

"Doming is very handsome," said the younger maid. "Do

you think his cousin Inday was as beautiful as Lady Adela?"

"No one is more beautiful than Lady Adela," said her older friend.

A sharp voice interrupted. "What are you girls doing, standing around clucking like chickens? You should have been done here half an hour ago." As the maids scurried back to work, the housekeeper's scolding continued. "Don't let me catch you gossiping about Chief Doming again! That's none of your business."

I heard a dozen conversations like that one, and a dozen more about Lady Adela, the Bagobo princess who was now Doming's wife.

In the early years before World War II, Magpet's people were mostly members of the Bagobo tribe. In the years before Doming, they were led by the highly respected, and extremely wealthy, Chief Igianon Latimbang. Igianon owned the entire town area and the neighboring villages, too. His lands extended beyond the mountainside bordering Magpet. There were lakes and rivers running through. Rubber was harvested, and coconuts. He owned rice plantations and animal farms. Members of the Bagobo tribe cultivated his lands for him. Adela was his daughter.

If Chief Doming's eldest daughter Erlinda was mysterious and fascinating to me, then Lady Adela, Erlinda's own mother, was as unapproachable as the sun itself.

As Chief Igianon's only child, Adela was heir to all his riches—raised with her every whim indulged, surrounded by servants. Her beauty was spoken of throughout Magpet, and she came into adulthood with multiple suitors eager for her hand. Most of them were predictably present and accounted for: the son of this or that family, the heir of this or that plantation. She loved the attention, but when she was honest with herself, she knew she was bored by them all.

There was only one man who intrigued her: a young man of mystery, extremely bright, a smooth talker, and much respected by her father. Plus, he was the best-looking of any suitor who had approached her. This was Doming Apostol. For some scandalous reason, Doming left his family lands behind in Cebu in the central Philippines, and came to Mindanao, seeking employment. The idea that Doming fled for his life from an outraged family was fascinating to the spoiled princess.

Having studied in Cebu to become a lawyer, Doming became a legal clerk and rapidly gained local business connections, making friends with many influential members of the Bagobo tribe. Quickly, the intelligent young man learned to speak the dialect, and understand all about the Bagobo ways of life. The Bagobo admired him and often sought his advice.

Chief Igianon needed a personal clerk to run his affairs. When introduced to Doming, Igianon knew this was the man for the job. Doming's education, intelligence, and quick-witted skills immediately earned Chief Igianon's trust and confidence. Soon, the chief had turned over the management of his entire estate to Doming.

Thus, Doming and Adela saw each other often. Doming's heart must have mended from the parting with Inday, for soon he became enamored with Adela's beauty, her fortune, or both. And why shouldn't he be?

Doming was a heartbreaker and knew how to make himself attractive. He played it smart with Adela and didn't come on too strong, intriguing Adela all the more. Usually, her suitors were eager to win her attention. This Doming was restrained, dignified. Adela always got what she wanted, and she determined that Doming was the person she would marry, not realizing that Doming had decided that himself the moment he had laid eyes on her.

Doming and Adela married in 1938. Chief Igianon died a few years later. All his wealth he left to his daughter and her husband. Doming Apostol became the new head of the Bagobo tribe, Lady Adela at his side.

I regarded Lady Adela with complete deference, even caution. I barely dared to look at her. For her part, she took very little notice of me. She dealt with the nanny when it came to issuing orders about the care of the children, and with the housekeeper when it came to matters of the household. Orders were passed down through the ranks, and eventually I knew what I was meant to do.

Yet I often held her own children in my arms.

Of course, Erlinda had little to do with me. And Dodong, the second child, was old enough that he did not need me, either. But at least he spoke to me, and was always polite and friendly. He knew that his younger siblings adored me. Dodong was so much like his father: smart, good-looking, strong-willed, and short-tempered. Everyone knew that Chief Doming had high aspirations for him, hoping that Dodong would take over the estate and become chief one day. Dodong, however, was not interested.

Maybe that was why Chief Doming focused so hard on Erlinda instead. Though she was a daughter, she was determined to follow in her father's path while Dodong painted and dreamed of being a sailor and traveling around the world. No matter how Chief Doming tried to involve Dodong, the boy resisted, daydreaming through lectures or dinner, or making himself impossible to find. Often their equally volatile tempers flared and they shouted at each other, frightening the younger children. Despite his frustration, Chief Doming loved Dodong. When they were not angry with each other, he'd compliment Dodong's intelligence and artistry, and even his stubbornness. "That's my son—just like me. No one tells him what to do!"

Next in age came Orlando, then Rodolfo, born one year apart. They were good, quiet boys, but both rather anxious. Their parents were busy, and as is sometimes the case with middle children, the boys were always in the shadow of the eldest siblings, Erlinda and Dodong. I remember Erlinda could get them to do anything with a word. They both wanted badly to please her. They tagged after her until she snapped at them to leave her alone. Sometimes Dodong played with them: he was the captain of the ship, and Orlando, Rodolfo, and Rachel were his crew.

Rachel was, of course, the next child. She was the sweetest little girl, as if her heart was just made for love. I adored her because she adored me. She looked very much like her mother. I imagined she would grow up to be just as beautiful, and I hoped that she would not become arrogant and dismissive when she became a great lady. I wished she would always stay a child so I could cuddle and play with her.

The two youngest Apostol children were also girls, Evelyn and Sarah. They, too, were put into my care, and became part of my heart.

Lady Adela's own babies grew up loving me, making my world a brighter place. Watching over them was my favorite duty. I never considered it a chore at all. I fed them, sang to them, and taught them how to play the games I had learned watching the village's children. I fussed when Rodolfo scraped his knee, or Rachel bumped her head.

Seizing every chance, I cherished the moments spent in the joyful company of Lady Adela's children. I pushed their tricycles from behind. I dressed their dolls and made them talk. I brushed hair, straightened socks, and taught them how to tie their shoelaces under the shade of the fruit trees. I was part of their daily lives.

It was strange that Lady Adela seldom looked my way, and stranger still that I never expected her to. This was the way of my life for many years, and except for a few desperate wishes, I was content to be there.

## CHAPTER FIVE

# ERLINDA'S BOOKS

Sometimes on pleasant days, Erlinda did her schoolwork in the yard. As I minded her little brothers and sisters, I watched from the corner of my eye as she pored over her beautiful books. When she turned to write in her notebook, her pencil flew across the page. To me, it looked like magic. I didn't know how to read or write.

Yet I had dreams of almost doing so, dreams in which I was seated on the warm lap of someone who loved me. A kind hand hovered, covering and guiding my much smaller one, showing me how to paint lines with a brush over a wide sheet of paper. Swoop, swish, swoop. A voice. "That is your name. Child of Joy. See how pretty it looks?" How I strained to see that symbol, to remember the word. But they, and the guiding hand, seemed to always wash away in a haze of red rain.

I was lower than the lowest class, a servant who had no right to envy anything. And I didn't dare...quite. But this was something I couldn't help. I envied Erlinda's ability to read and write. I wanted that for myself.

I wanted to be a girl who had time to sit on a warm afternoon, reading a book and writing on a sheet of clean paper. A maid brought Erlinda cold drinks, and cookies or sliced fruit on a plate. Often Erlinda sat there frowning slightly over her work until the light faded, only sometimes raising her head to look at her younger brothers and sisters while they played. She never looked directly at me.

I knew she was excellent at her schoolwork; everyone said so. I heard whispers of admiration about her intelligence and her competence. The servants thought of her as a worthy successor to Chief Doming. "That Erlinda is a genius. Do you know, she helps the Chief run his businesses?" the cook said. "I've heard she can do sums and read the newspapers better than he can!"

Erlinda quickly became more educated than her mother. Lady Adela never had any reason to apply herself to studies. I supposed she could read and write. She often threw out magazines that I took from the waste-bins and perused at night. Erlinda was her father's daughter, however. She was whip-smart, driven, and ambitious, just like him. She was not even a teenager before she was an active part of his business affairs. And he was obviously so proud of her. His face shone with it when he bragged about her to the guests who gathered in the privileged house. He let her come to business meetings and even encouraged her to speak. How I marveled at this, as I scurried around removing dirty plates and silverware, rushing these things back to the kitchen for washing.

On those afternoons when Erlinda worked on the patio, I could barely concentrate on minding the little ones. I followed after them making sure they were safe, but their chatter escaped me. Most of my attention was on Erlinda. I couldn't imagine what mysteries she was studying over there. Sometimes I played tag with the children hoping they would run close to her so I could glimpse what she was doing. But if they did dare to race closer, Erlinda always said, "Go away, you little brats, I'm busy," though her tone was gentle enough with them. In my direction, she snapped, "Keep them in the yard."

One day she left her books to go inside for something. I pretended to be searching for one of the babies' toys, and crept over to the patio to peer at her schoolwork, open on the table. The pages were fascinating. There were pictures of people in fancy clothes and printed words beneath them. Those printed words, I surmised, held the secrets of these people—their names, and why they deserved to be in a book. Were they kings or heroes? I looked at Erlinda's notebook and saw dozens more words there. I bit my lip, hardly able to grasp that a girl younger than me could know how to write so many words. They looked like impossibly complex patterns of lines and squiggles, yet I knew they all had meaning. It made my heart ache to think of how all that meaning was hidden from me.

"Diamon, Diamon!" called Rachel. "Come back! Watch

what I can do!"

I reluctantly left Erlinda's books behind. If I asked her, would she let me see one of them? I wondered if she would let me borrow one to look at before bedtime. I quashed the thought. Books were not for someone like me. Erlinda would never let me touch them. My hands were dirty. I might get in trouble for bothering her.

Even Erlinda's younger brothers, Dodong and Orlando, knew how to read. Rachel would soon be old enough for school, too. I knew they had children's books in their rooms, though they never brought them to the yard. Would it be possible for these little ones to teach me something—if I was clever about my request and disguised it under an offer to play? "Why don't you bring a book for us to look at?" I dared once to ask Orlando.

"Nanny says books can't come outside," Orlando told me. "They'll get torn up. Books are for bedtime."

He saw my disappointment and said, "But you can tell me a story if you want to."

Sweet boy, trying to ease my sadness. I said, "I'm sorry, Orlando. I don't know any stories."

That was not true. I knew some stories, but none that should be told to a little boy. I forgot I was a little girl and shouldn't have known them, either. I will tell you one now.

## CHAPTER SIX

# THE SINS OF WAR

Before going to Chief Doming's home, I was taught nothing about my place in the world except what I learned at the end of a kick, a jab, or an insult. Even when kinder people let me into their home, they knew little more about the world than I did, so even if I had been brave enough to ask direct questions, they could not have told me much.

World War II had left devastation in its path, both to the landscapes in which we lived and to the hearts of the people. I try to remember that when I think of how the sins of war were pinned on me, a blameless child. Yes, it was brutally unfair. War can make monsters of people. Forgiveness is so hard to achieve.

And forgetting? It is impossible.

When I was still simply a Magpet village trophy, other children sneered and shouted at me.

"*Japon*," they'd hiss.

They played a frightening game in which they pretended to be prisoners marching to death, goaded by terrifying soldier captors. And I was always the "Japon" even if I didn't want to be. They said I was forcing them to walk a thousand miles until they died, then either they rose up against me as valiant soldiers, and "stabbed me to death" with sticks, or their avenging ghosts came to haunt me after I'd left them to die on the road. They inevitably chased me.

I was tiny and I learned to be fast, but the big kids could usually catch me anyway, and if I were ordered to "stop," it seemed like I'd better stop or my punishment would be worse when finally caught. Usually I escaped with nothing but injured feelings, but I always had a few bruises on my arms and thighs. The physical injuries did not hurt as much as the way they looked at me, as if my face offended them. What did they mean? What had I done? I had never hurt anyone or anything, but it didn't matter to them.

Their accusations and games gave me horrible nightmares that did not seem to stop while I was awake. I trembled whenever forced to walk too close to groups of children. My only goal was to be ignored. I slipped through the village like an expert stealthy spy, keeping to shadows and behind walls.

Adults sometimes caught the kids in this wargame and scolded them fiercely, but usually their reprimand had nothing to do with me. I was simply a prop in a game the grownups disapproved of. The adult would say quite adamantly, "Don't mock the ghosts of our fallen. They'll never rest. You'll bring terrible luck on us." Some children were spanked or smacked on the head for playing the war game, and I couldn't help but feel satisfaction. But I would rather they'd left me alone to fetch the water from the river or find the person I'd been sent to find, or whatever task had sent me out on the paths that day.

That was my introduction to nationality. I did not understand it until years later.

When I went to live at the Apostol home, I was no longer victimized that way. I was seldom sent out beyond the grounds; when I did go, it was to run a quick errand. I had a bizarre and unwanted celebrity status, so everyone in Magpet knew where I worked by then. They had too much respect for Doming to interfere with one of his servants. It didn't stop them from hissing at me or staring, but at least the town children no longer hit or chased me.

As I have said, I kept my mouth closed and my ears open. It would have to be through listening if I was ever to learn anything. When Doming turned on his radio, I tried to move my work near a window so I could hear, whether it was news, music, or entertainment. I listened anytime Erlinda talked to her father about what she learned in school or what she'd read in the newspaper. I positioned myself as close as I could to anyone speaking about matters of the world.

What did I seek? What did I hope to understand?

Children see the world as theirs alone. They are born believing they are the center of the universe and that everything around them is simply part of the bubble in which they exist. As they grow older, they realize they are part of a community, town, or country. They learn their place in the world.

Communities have an order to them. Children fit into that order. They are part of families, circles of friends, and groups of students or playmates; that is how it should be. I saw other children growing into their roles and naturally wondered what I was growing into. Even though I was part of the Magpet community as its lowest member, I never belonged there. They made it clear daily that I was not one of them.

When Rachel was only a toddler, she received a wooden puzzle. It once had belonged to Erlinda and was passed down from sister to sister. On a wooden board were cutouts of six animals: pig, chicken, dog, caribou, duck, and cow. Each separate cutout animal fit perfectly into its place. I showed Rachel how to work it and made each animal's noise as I reconstructed them, making her giggle with my chicken clucking and duck quacking. I was not afraid to make noise around Rachel.

Now it was her turn. Little Rachel was eager to put the animals back on the board, but she didn't yet understand that each animal had its own particular spot. She strained with the puzzle piece and frowned. "Diamon, make it go!" she demanded, showing me the trouble.

"Miss Cow does not fit there," I told her. "No matter how hard you push. She'll never go into that spot." I thought, *I know just how Miss Cow feels.*

Surrounded by the usual trappings of a culture, I was yet utterly apart from it. My existence was an anomaly. I was not born there, or I didn't think so. I understood that once I must have had parents but that they were gone now. When I tried to remember why, I felt so sad and frightened that it was hard to piece the thoughts together in order. I remembered deaths, yes, but sometimes I wasn't sure if those deaths had been my parents, or someone else. Or maybe only one of them had died, and the other had escaped. Or maybe, maybe, maybe...

With joy and grief, I dreamed my family was alive and well somewhere, searching for me. One day, they might ride into Magpet in a long, beautiful car like nothing that had ever entered the town. I imagined a chauffeur opening the door for them. Emerging from their vehicle, they shone like couples I had glimpsed in magazines, dressed in spotless white clothing with hats tilted across their brows, shading their faces so I never quite saw their features. They announced, "We have come to retrieve our Diamond, our most beloved, intelligent child! Where is our Diamond?"

My dream parents had bodyguards like Doming's big men, who shoved away anyone who tried to stop me from running to my parents, and leaping into their car to be driven away to a mansion in Manila, or an even more exotic place where I would live like a princess, have a million books, wear clean bright clothes, and have a hot bath every day, and where I would attend school and learn more than Erlinda could ever know.

One of the hired nannies became displeased with me when she decided Orlando and Rachel liked me too much.

It annoyed her that they obeyed my gentle requests to finish their food, or wash their faces, when they wouldn't obey her snapped instructions.

She waited for a good moment when other people were out of earshot. Then she pursed her lips and told me she was from Davao, the largest and most populated city in Mindanao.

"I find it so interesting," she said, "that Davao was made into a city just because too many Japanese were living here. The Japons just kept coming, thinking they could make rules and make all this money and take over all the trade. They nested themselves around Port of Davao like rats, so thick they called it Little Japan. Well, we showed them who was in charge. They're not there anymore, are they? Don't you find that interesting?" She smiled smugly when she saw that her words confused and upset me.

I didn't know if she was telling the truth, but I heard that before World War II, a great many Japanese businesspeople came to live in Mindanao, because the economy could make them rich. And after the War? They had either been killed, or fled, or they pretended they were not Japanese anymore.

I kept silent on the matter. There was nothing for me to say that would help. I didn't dare defend the Japanese—first, I knew nothing of them, and second, it would lead to trouble for me. And I didn't dare declare myself a loyal Bagobo because others would call me a liar and say I wasn't good enough to be one of them.

Sometimes when my little charges heard rumors in the house or saw me get scolded or referred to as a "stupid Japon," they got bold enough to ask about me. Orlando simply blurted it out one day. “Diamon, are you a Japon?”

I was a bit frightened to answer him. If I said no, then he might tell his parents or nanny, and I could get in trouble for lying. If I said yes, then my little adopted family might think less of me. So I told him that I didn’t know. Rachel overheard, as did Rodolfo, and they joined in. These three were bright, and they knew I was different somehow from everyone else. Now was their chance to figure out why.

The questions continued. “What does it mean to be a Japon?”

I said, “I don’t know what it means.” They pursued the topic with the persistence of children, not tactless, but thoughtless, never realizing how hard it was for me to answer them. Though I evaded their questions, I knew that soon they would simply ask someone else, who would tell them the awful truth.

“I am just Diamond,” I insisted. “I don’t know what else or how else to be.”

But I was lucky in this. The children innocently loved me, and it seemed that no matter what else they heard, they continued to do so.

The Japanese invaded the Philippines in 1941. They attacked Clark Air Base in Pampanga just after they attacked Pearl Harbor, the battle that brought the United States into the war. Then the Japanese immediately began landing troops in Luzon. The Americans and Filipinos there fought them hard but, I was told, the Japanese did a "sneak" attack the Philippines' forces weren't prepared for.

General George MacArthur, the American leader stationed in the Philippines at the time, withdrew his troops to Bataan, to make sure that the beautiful, historic city of Manila wasn't destroyed. The Japanese occupation went on from 1942 until 1945. I learned that despite McArthur's efforts, Manila was destroyed anyway.

"They demolished our history hoping to make us forget," said one of the men who came to meet with Doming. He wasn't speaking to me when he said it, but I was gathering ashtrays and felt his eyes slide over me.

The bitter nanny told me her own version of events, saying, "Those Japanese invaders thought they could hide here. They thought that with the jungles and the heat, and the bad roads and the rain, that the American soldiers would never be able to find them. But the Americans sent troops on ships to help our warriors. We rousted them out. We ran them off. They won't dare ever come back here again." She examined me, as if she'd just realized something. "I suppose your family must have left you behind when they were running away. You might have been too heavy to carry."

Her words left me feeling cold and hollow.

"What she says is not true," I murmured to myself, when I was alone. "It was an accident. They did not mean to leave without me."

Still, I lifted Rachel and carried her around the yard, to see if a little girl truly was too heavy to carry. I tried to run with her, and she laughed as she bounced in my arms. I found I could not run very far or very fast with her weight;

I was unbalanced and quickly grew tired. I pressed on until my breath heaved out painfully. I had to stop and Rachel wriggled away from me.

So maybe it was true, after all.

CHAPTER SEVEN

# A KIND MISSIONARY

Christian missionaries often came to Magpet to minister to the people there. Chief Doming donated a parcel of land next to his own estate for the construction of a church so that there would be a central place of worship in the town. Other than Chief Doming's home and the cantina, the church served as the main gathering place for Magpet. I had to fetch things, food or messages or donations, for the Chief's people; errands to the church were part of that.

Brother Tim came along when I was about twelve years old, and at first his presence did not matter at all to me. He was simply the next face in a string of people who came to work at the church, and missionaries had never bothered to notice me before. When they came to converse with the Chief, I was just another servant in a great household. Servants were meant to be ignored, and I put extra effort into my invisibility.

As for the church itself, I rarely entered it on my own. My chores only took me into the storage building beside it when I was sent with food or supplies that Doming wanted the missionaries to have. There I normally encountered a local worker, someone who did the cooking and cleaning. She took my deliveries, loaded me down with things to return to the Apostol house, and shooed me away.

Shortly after the new missionary came, however, as I brought two baskets of vegetables to the storage room, I found him standing inside. What was he doing? Taking inventory, perhaps, or...was he waiting for me?

Brother Tim was a young man, I thought, with skin so pale he looked ill, and hair an amazing color like orange and yellow mixed. I thought he must be the ugliest man I'd ever seen, but he smiled at me warmly, scaring me as much as a shout would have. He looked pleased to see me, but I didn't know why.

"Hello there," he said. He spoke the language of Magpet but with an inflection that made him harder to understand. If I had not been so sharp a listener, I might have never grasped his words. But I heard everything. He said, "I'm Brother Tim. What's your name?"

I was not permitted to ignore a direct question. "Diamond," I whispered with my eyes downturned, setting down my load.

"I'm sorry, what did you say? I couldn't hear you."

"Diamond," I tried to speak a little louder, but it was hard. My voice had learned that quiet was best. I didn't want to get in trouble.

"Diamond! That's a beautiful name. What did you bring for me?" He came close, peering into the baskets. "Sweet potatoes and carrots for my dinner. Please thank Chief Doming."

I found it bizarre for Brother Tim to imagine that I ever was allowed to address Chief Doming. But again, I wanted no trouble. I nodded my head in agreement, ready to bolt back out the door. Then I realized I couldn't go yet. He was new, and I had to make certain he knew about the baskets. If he misplaced or took them, I'd have to endure a tongue-lashing from the cook. So I steeled myself and spoke as clearly as I could, "I'll fetch back the baskets tomorrow."

"Thank you so much. Wait a moment, Diamond. Won't you stay and talk to me?"

I wanted nothing more than to run, but I knew better than to disobey commands. I stood with my head bowed, waiting.

"You work for Chief Doming?" asked Brother Tim. I nodded. "And...your parents, do they work there as well?"

I shook my head.

He was not surprised by my answer. I had the feeling that he already knew, or at least suspected, many of the facts about my life. "Where are your parents, Diamond? Do they live nearby?"

I shook my head once more.

Brother Tim crouched down a bit, so that I was forced to look into his strange, pale face. I averted my eyes quickly. What had I done to deserve his scrutiny.

"I'm scaring you, aren't I?" he asked. "Don't be afraid. I

want to be your friend."

No one had ever suggested friendship with me. It was ridiculous. He was going to do something cruel in just a moment. Maybe he did not know yet that I was a Japon. When he found out—

"You're Japanese, aren't you?" he asked.

My heart fell. My freakishness was so obvious that he was able to guess. Ah, well, it was best to admit it right away, and get it over with, so I nodded once more.

He said something in a different language. Then he said, "You are one of the many orphans from the War, I'll wager. How on earth did you come to be here?"

I had plenty of theories about that—the myriad of variations I had heard from the people in Magpet, and the few I had imagined on my own. I was unwilling to tell him any of them. What I said was, "I don't know."

He might have seen the sheer distress on my face because he let me leave. "See you tomorrow," he said cheerfully. I thought he was mocking me.

I had not counted on the determination of Brother Tim. Not that day, but in the days that followed, he pulled the truth from me, or at least, as much of the truth as I knew. He must have asked others about me, too. Each time I brought the food for the church, or retrieved the baskets, or carried a message, he stopped me and spoke to me, prodding and poking at my meager, young life.

At first he terrified me. Then he angered me, because I was certain any day now he would show his true colors and mock me, giving me something new to fear. In my careful listening to what others said, I heard nothing but good things about Brother Tim: that he was wise and kind, that he took a great interest in the people of Magpet.

Then, after my seventh or eighth visit, I felt something different. He asked a question and I wanted to answer him. Nobody ever asked me anything, except the children, and their questions were usually nonsense or simply about what they could or couldn't do or have. Brother Tim asked me something astonishing. "Do you speak any Japanese?"

I found that, when I answered, I was able to look directly into his face. He did not seem as ugly to me now as he had before. He was only different-looking, and his coloring was becoming more interesting than bizarre. I longed to ask him if that crop of orange was his real hair.

To answer his question, I counted for him in Japanese, faltering after ten. Then I said, "Those are the numbers, I think. That's all."

Brother Tim looked thoughtful for a while. Then he said, "I believe that life has been very difficult for you here."

"No, sir. No, sir," I assured him vehemently. Oh mercy, I couldn't have word getting back to the Apostol household that I had any complaints. I couldn't be sent back into the village, away from my little adopted family of children and the only place I'd ever been truly safe. My previous guardians would take me in; they were still nearby, always friendly and glad to see me. But they certainly could not protect me from the likes of Datu, and how dreadfully I would miss the Apostol children!

I assured Brother Tim quite seriously, "Chief Doming's

house is a fine place. I am very happy there. I am honored to work for the Chief."

He motioned for me to calm down, another gesture that I couldn't understand. Whatever could he want from me? He said, "I suppose you have been working for many years. Probably since you can remember. Have they ever let you go to school?"

I started a bit at the word. Could he see my thoughts? Saying the right thing was important. "No sir. School is not for…servants."

"Can you read?" he asked.

I felt suddenly and alarmingly close to tears. Speaking with someone kind and gentle, who asked about the one thing I dared to want was more than I could handle. I had to duck my head away again to hide my face.

Brother Tim wasn't easily fooled. "It's all right, you know. Some people get to be quite old before learning to read; it's nothing to be ashamed of. I could teach you how. I have some books, and we could study a bit in the evenings."

"No," I said in a strangled voice. "I have chores. The babies have to be put to bed. I have…"

"Perhaps," said Brother Tim, "I will speak to Doming about letting you come by a few times a week. Everyone should learn to read. It's one of life's great pleasures."

Great pleasures? I didn't understand what that meant. Was life supposed to have "great pleasures"?

He recognized my bafflement and rephrased, "It's an important skill. It will make you a better worker. That's the truth. He'll see reason, I'm sure. Doming is very intelligent."

I do not know who Brother Tim spoke with, or what he might have said. But suddenly the staff knew that on a few mornings each week, I was permitted to linger for a half-hour at the church for lessons. The cook believed I would receive "Bible lessons," and of course she had something snide to say about what good they might do for me.

I didn't care what she thought. The first morning I sat beside Brother Tim at his kitchen table, he gave me a small chalkboard and chalk. He wrote something on it first, saying as he did, "D-I-A-M-O-N-D. That is how you spell your name. There are seven letters in it, see, and the first and last are the same, the D-sound. Let me show you how to draw them."

This was miraculous. Brother Tim guided my hand, showing me how to shape the letters on the chalkboard. Then he traced my name very faintly on the board and allowed me to trace over it repeatedly. We said the letters aloud as I drew them. I had only ever drawn in the dirt before. I enjoyed the luxury of the chalk and the slate. I pressed too hard and broke a stick of chalk. I looked up in alarm. Brother Tim just shrugged and handed me another. "It's only chalk, Diamond. It's all right."

I concentrated so hard on those letters that the time raced by, and suddenly Brother Tim said, "That's all for today. Would you like to try to write it all by yourself before you go?"

He wiped the board clean. My heart gave a sick little lurch when my name disappeared. I took the chalk determinedly in my fingers and wrote the symbols he had shown me. I called the letters aloud as I carefully created them.

"That's very good!" Brother Tim exclaimed. "You're so smart, Diamond!"

I blushed with pleasure at the compliment. I didn't know the words to say what I felt. I had been waiting, for as long as I could remember, to know how to read and write. My eyes, fingers, and mind were ravenous for this information. They grabbed hold and would not let go.

"We'll practice letters on this slate because it can be used again and again," he told me as I reluctantly left. "But when you get to be a very good writer, we'll get some pencils and paper for you."

CHAPTER EIGHT

# WONDERFUL AND TERRIBLE LESSONS

Now that I had unlocked the secret of my name, I was terrified of losing it again. I drew it everywhere I could—in the garden's dirt while I watched the children, in the air as I lay in bed at night. I was half-sick with eagerness to return to Brother Tim's table and learn more.

On the days when I had no lessons, they were all I thought about. When I was with the children in the yard, I gave them sticks so we could all write together. The little ones did not notice I could suddenly write my name, but Erlinda noticed quickly enough. She appeared suddenly behind me and scared me half to death with her brittle laughter.

"Oh, aren't you clever?" she said, examining my work. A few moments ago I'd been proud of my penmanship. Now with Erlinda peering down, I suddenly found my letters blocky and clumsy; they looked no better than Rachel's awkward scrawls.

Erlinda murmured, "Our missionary is so kind to teach the lower classes. I wonder what good it will do. The 'A' is wrong, by the way. And the 'M' and 'N' look too much the same. Nobody will be able to read that. Here's the right way to do it." She took Rachel's stick and wrote across the ground in a script I couldn't decipher, moving fast and sending dirt scattering. "That's how *adults* write their names." She walked away, sighing as if giving me advice had simply worn her out.

Brother Tim read to me from his Bible, and from some other books too. He had books with pictures in them, as nice as any Erlinda owned. He let me dawdle over the pages for as long as I wanted and answered all my questions. At first I was afraid to ask but he was so kind to me that soon I was hardly done hearing one answer before I asked another question.

"How many books are there in the world? What kinds of things do people read about? Why are there sometimes pictures, but sometimes not? Who writes the books that people read? Who teaches them how to do it?"

I pointed to letters on the page and said, "That is a 'D' like in Diamond, right?" and Brother Tim applauded and said, "Good job! Can you find any of the other letters in your name?" I found them fast, making few errors.

Brother Tim read me the story of a terrible flood and

Noah, who made a boat big enough to hold two of every animal in the world. The story fascinated me because sometimes during Magpet summers it rained so hard it seemed the sky was falling. Water stood inches deep in the roads, and ditches turned into rivers that were hard to cross. During these typhoons, the wind blew viciously, tearing apart plants and fences and the cheaper huts and structures in town. Picking up after the storms was a regular part of Magpet life.

"Will we have a flood like that here?" I wanted to know. The idea seemed awful...but not as awful as it should have. I had a brief, gleeful idea of Magpet being demolished beneath the waves.

Brother Tim assured me, however, that there would be no more floods to cover the world, that God had promised us this in the Bible.

"If there was a flood that covered Magpet," I said, "I would rescue all the Apostol children—Dodong, Orlando, Rodolfo, Rachel, Evelyn and baby Sarah—and I would escape with them on a boat."

"Hmm," said Brother Tim, counting. "I suppose Erlinda is old enough to look after herself."

"Erlinda doesn't need my help with anything," I said quickly to cover my mistake. "But I wouldn't leave anyone behind. Not even if..." I thought for a moment as to how I might phrase my question. "Brother Tim, are little children hard to carry if you are trying to run? I tried running with Rachel in my arms, and it was awfully hard to do. I'm only worried that I might drop them accidentally, if they are too heavy, and leave them behind."

Brother Tim thought about this for a much longer time than I expected him to. Suddenly he gazed right into my face. I was accustomed now to his examinations of me, and they no longer made me afraid. Brother Tim did not hate the way I looked. In fact, he liked my face very much, especially when he could make me smile.

"Diamond," he said after a long while. "Your parents did not drop you or leave you accidentally. If there was any way that they could have escaped with you, they would have done it. It was wartime, and wartime means that terrible things can happen, even to children. But I am positive that they loved you. They are in Heaven now, watching over you, and they still love you very much."

I was overcome with a mixture of feelings. Brother Tim was the one person I knew who always told me the truth. It was not that other people intentionally lied to me, but often their answers were tainted with dislike for my race or simple ignorance. If Brother Tim believed that my parents were in Heaven, that meant they were dead and would never be able to come and find me. That disappointment, however, was mild compared to the burden of worry I had carried. It had only been a fantasy to believe that my parents might be alive somewhere. Far more, I was relieved at his assurance that my parents would never have intentionally left me behind in this place.

For a brief time, I had things I had only dreamed of before: lessons, and books, and a friend. I gobbled up everything Brother Tim could tell me. I wrote my name a hundred times on the slate. I pushed through page after page of books, asking him about everything. He laughed at my eagerness and said, "Diamond, we'll never get through the alphabet if you keep jumping ahead!" I wanted more time for lessons, but the other servants were always cross when I returned, saying that they had to work twice as hard to make up for my absence. I was afraid they would tell Chief Doming or Lady Adela, and my lessons would end.

However, it was not the ire of the other servants or the orders of the Chief that ended my short education.

Early one day, the cook remarked to me, "So I hear we'll have you back in the mornings now. Your missionary is being replaced."

I thought, certainly, she must be goading me. I must have dared to look as if I might argue with her, because she assured me, "Oh, you can ask him yourself—if you can catch him before his bus comes. His church ran out of money. Or maybe they think he's wasting his time here. I have an idea! Why don't you ask him to take you along?"

It was not a lessons day, and I had no excuse to go to the church. It was just next door, yet if I neglected any of my chores, I would most certainly be reprimanded. A scolding meant little to me; I'd endured them for years. Fear of banishment from the house was what made me frantic to be compliant and good. So I suffered through that day and the next, longing for an excuse to hurry to Brother Tim.

By the time I was actually able to do so, I had confirmation of his impending departure from three other people. I heard the maids talking, and I even heard Doming say so at dinner: "Brother Tim is leaving us to go to an African mission." Nobody mentioned his friendship with me. They didn't know about it or didn't care.

I got to see my friend one last time. I had already cried all my tears silently the night before, and on the day of our last lesson I arrived with swollen eyes and a broken heart. Brother Tim exclaimed over me. "Oh thank goodness, here you are. I thought I'd have to come to the house and ask to see you, because I could not leave without saying goodbye. Diamond, I'm so sorry. I had no idea I'd be called away so soon."

"Why do you have to go?" I whispered.

"It's my job to go where God and my church tell me," he replied. "It's my calling. Look, I'll leave word with the next missionary that you are a very good student...and maybe he will have time to continue your lessons."

Unaccustomed to arguing, I just nodded mutely. I didn't want another missionary. None of the other missionaries had ever had time for me. I wanted Brother Tim, my friend, to stay.

"Diamonds are the hardest substance in the world," said Brother Tim, "and they're the most beautiful, too. You are strong and beautiful like a diamond. God loves you, cares for you, and has a wonderful plan for you. Don't lose hope, Diamond. Your life has a purpose. I want you to find happiness in what you do."

Again, I nodded.

"Even if you're angry with me, will you remember what I've said?" he asked.

"I'm not angry," I said. "I'm really not. I'm so sad I could die."

He smiled, which surprised me. "I'm sad too, but neither of us is going to die from it. We will always be friends of the heart. Promise you believe me, and will remember what I said. God loves you."

"I promise to remember," I told Brother Tim. And I always did. He left with his books and his lessons, the slate and the chalk, his kind smile, and his bright hair. But he had taught me how to write my name, and given me some hope to cling to: God ensured that my life had a purpose. I kept those gifts for the rest of my life.

## CHAPTER NINE

# CHIEF DOMING IMPRISONED

In the great Apostol house in the center of Magpet, the children of the Chief and Lady Adela had their birthday parties in the main hall. These celebrations were favorites of mine, for many reasons. The house was always festive, the room decorated with bright tablecloths and napkins, and everyone was in a happy mood.

I was good with the children, so inevitably I would be needed close by to make certain they were looked after and behaving themselves, and not breaking out into little spats when their siblings got more attention for being the "birthday guest of honor." But they were such good children it was no trouble at all.

I got to watch the parties from up close, where I could see the presents, the birthday cake and treats, and enjoy the songs and the decorations. I almost dared to pretend I was part of the family at these times.

I did not enjoy Erlinda's birthday parties as much. As I've said, it was not exactly envy that ate at me, but bafflement. We were too close in age, so inevitably I compared her life to mine. Her birthdays were somehow more special, because she was the oldest child and Doming adored her. I did not even know my own birthdate.

At Erlinda's most recent birthday, when Chief Doming complimented her for turning into such a fine young lady, it struck me: this could be my birthday, too. Or my birthday might be tomorrow, or maybe it was yesterday. This realization landed on me so hard that I stood still for a moment too long, lost in thought, until Erlinda noticed. She smirked at me, saying, "Wake up and do your job. The boys are getting into everything."

They weren't, not really; they'd just gotten hold of some streamers and were whipping at each other with them. But I felt the eyes of everyone on me, particularly the girls invited from Erlinda's school. They gazed at me with their bright, clean faces, expectantly waiting for the servant to do as she was told. My own face burned as I turned away to corral the boys.

In 1954, the year when Baby Sarah was born, I was around sixteen years old. I had only a few months to come to know her before the household was sent into upheaval.

Because he owned so much of the land in and around

Magpet, Chief Doming employed a great many people and was their landlord, too. His intelligence was tinged with arrogance, and his short temper was widely known. Strict with his tenants, he expected hard work, unquestioning loyalty, and good productivity from them. Normally, no one dared to oppose him.

But there came a day when that changed.

The day had been quite ordinary for me until after Rachel and Evelyn had their lunch. I led them upstairs for naptime, putting them into the hands of their nanny. She got to sit quietly beside their beds as they napped, whereas I was expected to go to the kitchen and wash dishes. I ignored her smirking and returned downstairs to pump the sink full of water and begin. The sooner the dishes were done, the sooner I could start cutting up produce, which was one of my favorite chores. I enjoyed the food's beautiful smells and colors, and it was usually all right for me to have a few pieces for myself.

However, strange isolation and quiet met me downstairs. There was no one else in the kitchen, and the lunch dishes were not yet gathered from the table. This was unusual. I started my work and was up to my elbows in water and soap when I looked out the kitchen window to see that no one was working outside, either. Normally there were at least two or three workers visible, tending the lawn, trees, or gardens that sprawled across the house's backyard.

I worked for a few minutes more but finally could no longer stand the mystery. What if something was wrong? What if someone was sick or hurt? I couldn't imagine why

I was alone in the house. So I dried my hands on my apron and went cautiously looking for the rest of the servants.

I found them without much trouble, for as soon as I approached the front rooms of the house, I could hear voices outside. I went to the window to investigate. All the inside and outside servants were on the great house's driveway, talking quietly in bunches. There were townspeople scattered among them. Every few seconds they raised their heads to look toward a woman in the center of the yard. I realized it was Lady Adela herself they looked at. She spoke desperately with two Bagobo tribesmen who had been in the house many times before. As she urgently addressed them, I saw her wringing her hands and wiping tears from her face.

*Someone has died!* I thought. *Is it the chief? If the chief has died, will I be sent back into the town? What will happen to my little adopted family of Apostol children?*

I did not want to go out there, yet from inside the house, I couldn't hear anything. So I slipped out the front door and made myself small and unnoticeable, moving to the outskirts of the group where the housemaids gathered. I knew by now that if I wanted information, the housemaids were the ones to listen to.

"—just can't believe it!" one was exclaiming. "What will we do? Will there be a new chief?"

"They could send him to the electric chair," said one of the men from town, trying to frighten the maids.

"They wouldn't dare!" said another maid proudly.

"But wasn't he in the right?" demanded another maid. "They're his tenants. They *must* do what he says."

"He can't just go around shooting people for disobeying," the man from town responded. "That's too much! Those men are dead. They had families depending on them."

"Then they should have done their jobs and respected the Chief," the maid retorted hotly. "I don't feel one bit sorry for them."

"Oh poor Lady Adela!" the first maid whispered. "She'll likely die of a broken heart if her husband is executed."

I listened with growing horror and amazement as I put the pieces of the story together. Some of Doming's tenants working in the fields had disobeyed and openly disrespected him. They had no qualms about upsetting his legendary temper, which was their mistake. Doming came home just long enough to get his gun, then returned to the field and shot them all dead. It would later be confirmed that he killed three men that day, but at that moment, the rumors in the yard were exaggerated, crediting him with killing as many as eight.

The Bagobo tribal leaders came to inform Lady Adela that Chief Doming had surrendered himself to the police authorities in a neighboring town and was currently on his way to jail in Davao. They said there would be something called a "court hearing" to determine his guilt and punishment. The stories in the yard were riddled with speculation. Some said the Chief would be put in an electric chair, or at least that he would be imprisoned for the rest of his life, while others murmured that he would instead be fined, forgiven, or awarded a medal for his strong leadership.

Erlinda, Dodong, Orlando, and Rodolfo were brought

home early from school, bodyguards surrounding them. The boys looked pale and fearful, and even Erlinda seemed unsteady. I almost felt sorry for her. First they rushed to their mother. Lady Adela stared at the stricken children as if she hardly recognized them. Then Erlinda pushed her way in between her mother and the tribe leaders and began questioning them. Lady Adela stood aside and listened with her hands covering her lovely face. The boys tried to grasp their mother, but she gestured for them to go away.

The boys glanced around the yard until their eyes found me, and they came running. Orlando and Rodolfo nearly knocked me over with their desperate hugs, and clung to me, sobbing. Dodong stood close by, asking me what was happening, and what they should do. I had no answers for them. Nothing would ever be the same again.

For days we waited on tenterhooks to learn what might happen next. Lady Adela and Erlinda went away, I assumed to be near Chief Doming and hear his indictment.

Schedules were completely disrupted. The children missed school, staying at home so they wouldn't be subject to rumors and gossip. Meals were haphazard. We, the servants, were so accustomed to serving the Apostol family and then eating afterward that, without them in the house, we hardly knew how to function. Finally, the cook just made big pots of porridges or stews, and the servants came in when they were hungry and stood around blowing on the steaming contents, guessing about what horrors were coming. The servants were only too happy to stand around and gossip, and no amount of scolding or shouting would get them working again.

I had a new job, though it was one that no one had assigned me. I became the touchstone and substitute parent for the younger children. The nanny was willing to look after Evelyn and Sarah because they were too little to ask questions, but she had no patience for Rodolfo, Orlando, or Rachel, who urgently wanted to know where papa was, and where mama was, and why Erlinda got to go with mama, and when everyone would come back home again. She sent them to me, and so they became mine day and night.

Rodolfo, Orlando, and Rachel were always at hand, their eyes on me as if they feared I might vanish like their parents had. Even Dodong, who was old enough to take care of himself, stayed nearby. Of course, they heard the stories—these servants were never careful about talking around the children—and so they riddled me with questions I could not know the answers to. "Diamond, will Papa be killed? What happened? Why did he shoot the men? Is Mama mad at him?" Poor little Rachel was in misery, and meanwhile the boys went wild, tearing around the house and shouting up a storm, unable to sit still for more than a few moments at a time.

"Keep them quiet!" the housekeeper barked at me when the three boys went flying by her, growling like jungle tigers. "Aren't you supposed to be watching them?."

"They're just playing," I told her.

"Playing like savages," she sniped. "They should have

some respect for this tragedy. If I catch that Rodolfo howling again, I'll snatch him bald."

"You leave him alone! He's worried about his papa!"

She stared at me in amazement. I realized it was the first time I'd ever spoken back to her. I would never have said a thing on my own behalf, but my heart was breaking for my little ones. They had grown up with wonderful, beautiful parents, something I remembered only in dreams, and now they, like me, were alone. I couldn't bear the thought of it.

To my surprise, the housekeeper didn't scold me. Instead she looked rebuked and turned away, muttering, "If they're going to scream so, at least take them outside."

The next time I managed to gather the four of them together, I served bowls of the stew that the cook had made that day, and there was even rice. We sat at the table outside, where Erlinda often did her schoolwork, and we looked like a proper, if miniaturized, family. The children's appetites were poor. Only Dodong wanted to eat anything; the rest only picked at their food.

"I have an idea for you," I told them all. "While your mama and papa are away, you can pretend that I'm your mama. And we can play house together."

"I heard Papa was never coming back again," said Orlando, which made Rachel stab morosely at her stew.

"You shut up," Dodong ordered him.

"Stop it now," I said, but very gently. "If we're going to play house, we all have to be kind to each other. Dodong, you are the oldest boy so you have to be the nicest of all, and act like a grown man like your papa. Orlando and Rodolfo, you have to be good brothers to Rachel."

From my time in the village, I remembered what mothers there did for their children. I could be nothing like Lady Adela, but I was sure I could behave like a village mother. I said, "While I'm mama, I will make your dinners, and clean your clothes, and take care of you."

These were things I did already, but the children, and Rachel especially, seemed relieved to hear me say it aloud. They feared that if their parents could go away, anyone could. So for a few days while Chief Doming's fate was decided, we agreed to pretend together.

Chief Doming was not electrocuted. In his indictment, he pled guilty to the murder of the three men. Since he had turned himself in, the law was more forgiving. He was sent to the Philippines' largest penitentiary, located far away in Manila. To me, it sounded as if he was sent to another world.

An exhausted Lady Adela and an angry Erlinda returned home. The servants all scrambled back to work as soon as they heard Lady Adela was on the way, trying to fix the disarray that had built up in her few days' absence.

But Lady Adela was not the one they needed to worry about. She at once went to her room and barred the door, and we saw nothing of her for days. Erlinda, on the other hand, took charge of the home. The first thing I heard from her was admonishments about how bad the yard looked—and if the outside laborers didn't get busy, they could find work elsewhere. Now that her father was "away," she told them, she had no hesitation about firing lazy workers, to save him money.

Her threats and authority worked for a while, but not even one as strong as Erlinda could weather the storm that fast approached the Apostol household.

## CHAPTER TEN

# WHERE IS MY MAMA?

Chief Doming's incarceration left the estate in shambles. Lady Adela and Erlinda did what they could to keep things running, but quickly it became apparent that they could not take his place. Adela was absolutely unaccustomed to working; the scope of her husband's responsibilities overwhelmed her. Only a few times did she look over the ledgers or mail, and then she gave up. She took refuge in either sleeping the day away or disappearing from the house. At first, she might be gone for several hours, then half a day, and before long, entire nights would pass without her sleeping in her bed.

Erlinda was actually capable of much, and she understood a great deal about her father's business. Her influence was limited, though, because she was still a girl, and the tribe leaders would not take orders from her. I believe she did her best, and I admired her for it. Her braininess and determination always amazed me. Regardless, the tribesmen began to run their affairs on their own. Rent money became ever more sporadic as tenants realized they no longer had to pay the Chief. Someone from the tribe might have been collecting the money and using it elsewhere; I do not know.

I just know that many of the Apostol home's luxuries began to disappear. There were no longer fresh flowers for dinner tables, or sparkling, new bottles of liquor to serve to guests. There were no guests, either, except sometimes when tribe leaders came to the house to collect something. The children received no new toys or clothes. There were no special treats for them. Celebrations and parties ceased. Servants began to disappear from the house. Erlinda fired some of them; others left because they could see that the money was vanishing and knew that their jobs would not last much longer.

What exactly happened with the Bagobo tribe and the estate in those months, I can only guess, because my time was filled with caring for the children. The Davao nanny certainly did not stay long; she said her goodbyes and returned home only a couple of weeks after things fell apart. I was far happier without her; she had never liked me and took every opportunity to make me feel stupid or useless. I definitely saw her departure as a silver lining.

With fewer and fewer servants every week, I had both more to do for the little ones, and less to do elsewhere in the home. I still took care of things like laundry, cleaning, and dishwashing, but no longer did we have to prepare huge meals for tribal gatherings, or keep the main hall gleaming and spotless.

Seldom was I instructed to do anything anymore, but I saw at once that if I did not care for the children, no one would. Lady Adela was inconsolable (and unaccustomed to the chores of childrearing anyway), and Erlinda, barely more than a child herself, had taken on the huge burden of trying to keep the estate running in her father's place.

I was not, and had never been, a paid servant. I worked for a bed to sleep in, hand-me-down clothes, and a place at the table—and, mostly, to avoid being put back into the crowd of Magpet. I still had dark, lonely dreams about my early years surviving that cruelty.

As such, I could not be "fired" from the Apostol household exactly, only sent away if I displeased someone. I certainly had no desire to leave. The people I loved were in this house. I worked constantly to keep my little ones as well as I could. Adjusting to the absence of their father, and the mourning and distance of their mother, was difficult for all of them.

What I knew from my own life was that children crave consistency and security. All I could do in the meantime was to be their steady caring mama, and love them, and let them know that I would not leave. Instinct told me this would have to be enough.

In the back of my mind, I hoped that things would improve, that Lady Adela might snap out of her grief and begin to work, or hire someone to take over the estate. Erlinda might gain enough respect and skill to run things all on her own. The income might return. Somehow things would get back to normal. I prayed for that at night.

One day, Lady Adela was gone. Now, she had been out of the house so frequently, and was so withdrawn when she was home, that I might not have noticed except that Evelyn and Sarah were gone as well. She took her two youngest children and left. When I saw their empty beds, my heart wrenched. I imagined their fear and confusion at being suddenly pulled from the only home they'd ever known. I knew that something similar had happened to me when I was close to Evelyn's age. I thought, *at least she is still with her mama, and hopefully that makes her less afraid.*

Then I heard the rumors start again. Of the minimal servants remaining, there were still enough to gossip. "Her clothes are gone," I heard one say. "She took everything of value with her," said another. "Her jewelry, and the painting Chief Doming gave her, and the silver."

Everything of value? She took precious Evelyn and Sarah, but left behind her five oldest children!

"She has a man in Calinan," I heard the servants say. "He promised to take care of her."

And other low whispers: "A woman that beautiful has no trouble finding a man. I wouldn't wait around for a husband in prison, either."

"I've heard she's had that man for a long time. Long before the Chief was imprisoned."

"That's ridiculous. The Chief would never have allowed—"

"Some say the Calinan lover is the father of at least one of her children."

"If the Chief were still here, he'd kill her!"

"Shh, don't say such things! Erlinda will hear about it."

"All of you stop this immediately! Have some respect for the people who provide the roof over your head!"

"They're not providing anything now, are they? I haven't been paid in weeks."

*Lady Adela will be back soon*, I told myself. *This is her home; these are her children.*

But I was wrong. Days went by and then weeks, and she did not return.

It was simply terrible for the ones she left behind. Their father's absence was bad enough, and he had not left them intentionally. But how was I to explain that their mother had chosen to run away? Dodong and Orlando clearly missed her, yet they were old enough that at least they accepted the truth. Rodolfo and Rachel, on the other hand, were still young enough that they could not understand, and in their terror, they rarely left my side.

"Where is my mama?" Rachel asked me incessantly. My poor girl sat each day on the doorstep, watching the long road for her mother's return. When I joined her there to place my arm around her, Rachel sometimes sobbed, "Maybe she'll come home today. Why didn't she take me with her, Diamond? Maybe I didn't matter to her."

My heart ached for little Rachel. Deep sadness filled her, knowing that her mother had abandoned her without so much as an explanation. I wished I could do something to make it all better, but no matter how hard I tried, I couldn't find the right words to ease her pain. I fought back tears as I did my best to comfort her, telling her that everything would be alright and that her mother would return soon enough. But inside me, there lay a heavy feeling, one which said otherwise: that we might not see Lady Adela again.

When Rachel, Dodong, Orlando, Rodolfo, and I gathered for our meals in the evenings, I reminded them all that we were playing house, that I would continue to be their mama for now. I meant it completely. The longer their parents were away, the more dedicated I became to the children. No more did I consider them my adopted family—they *were* my family. And even if I told them repeatedly to remember that we were "playing house," in my mind, I was responsible for the Apostol children. They were as good as mine.

I remembered when Brother Tim told me that God had a wonderful plan for my life. Perhaps this was it. Here, I was badly needed. Though the situation was difficult, I actually felt more useful than ever before. I had an important responsibility.

Erlinda did care about her younger siblings. Still, she was under tremendous stress. Doming wrote to her from prison, telling her to find her mother and her baby sisters and bring them home. I do not know if his tone was pleading or threatening. I do not know what Erlinda did. Possibly, she went to Calinan to talk to her mother, or wrote letters.

Something must have changed because one day, Evelyn was brought back home again. Lady Adela sent the child back as an appeasement. Her siblings and I were overjoyed to see her, and the little girl was happy to be home once more. Being whisked away to Calinan had confused and frightened her.

Yet now, as with the other children, she realized her mother would not return. And the baby, Sarah, was still gone.

Finally, Erlinda left us, too, and I cannot truly blame her for it. She was in an impossible situation, and clever as she was, she found a way out. She received a marriage proposal from a local man called Rudy. Rudy came from a family that owned a vast expanse of land, so he had been blessed with the opportunity to live a life of comfort and privilege. Though she was only about fifteen years old, Erlinda accepted. She married and went to live with her husband.

With both Erlinda and Lady Adela gone, whatever was left of the estate's management disappeared. The workers were mostly gone as well. There I was, in this sprawling, nearly empty house, with no money, no instructions, and five children who looked to me to take care of them. We had nothing.

The day came when the kitchen was empty, the cupboards bare. With Rodolfo and Rachel tagging along, I went out to the yard and began gathering what fruits and vegetables were left. Then I realized that I must plant more, if we were to have anything to eat. So I planted the seeds I could harvest, and every day I worked in the cloying heat of the garden to keep us fed. Dodong and Orlando helped when they could. Even little Evelyn patted at the soil, mimicking her older siblings.

I had always been thin; now I grew even thinner as I toiled. Often I gave up portions of my own food to the children so they would not be so hungry. I remember many hot afternoons with the six of us sweating beneath the intense sun, weeding, picking, and digging away just so we'd have something for dinner. No one else would do it for us.

CHAPTER ELEVEN

# GOOD BEHAVIOR

After three years of incarceration, Chief Doming was released from prison for good behavior. He came home to find his estate in complete chaos. Surely it was difficult for him to see the depths to which his home and family had fallen.

Initially, there was joy. We learned from Erlinda that Chief Doming was on his way back. I did what I could to prepare a nice meal with the food that I scavenged from our small garden, but certainly, there would be no party or celebration. Dodong painted his father a "welcome home" picture with good renditions of the children's smiling faces on it. Orlando, Rodolfo, and Rachel made paper flowers for a centerpiece. We set up in the downstairs hall at the big table, which used to seat twenty or more guests. Little was left in the room but the table and chairs themselves. Much of the décor had been stolen by departing servants, or sold by Erlinda or Dodong to cover expenses.

Evelyn was anxious about all this; she did not seem to remember her father at all. She asked question upon question about "Papa" and what he was like and told me, "Mama says Papa is a brute and a fool." Her earnest little face was set just like her mother's when she said it, but I don't think she really understood what it all meant.

The Chief came home and walked in with two other Bagobo men. He looked ten years older than the last time I had seen him; he had grown thin and hard, with dark circles and heavy bags under his eyes.

Erlinda and her husband Rudy were joining us at the house for the Chief's return, and Erlinda raced to her father to embrace him. "Papa, Papa," she cried. "I've missed you so much!" Then the other children, emboldened by her forwardness, went tumbling toward him too–except for Evelyn, who stayed behind me, peering out fearfully.

Chief Doming hugged and then looked at each of his children individually, complimenting them so that they beamed with pride. "Dodong, you're a heartbreaker! Rodolfo, how tall you've gotten! Orlando, you have the shoulders of a giant! My Rachel is becoming a beautiful young lady. And of course, Erlinda is quite a mature, married woman now. I'm so happy to see you all." His face shone with the love he had for them; it made my heart pound with a mixture of happiness and grief, for I feared that I might no longer be needed.

The Chief approached me cautiously, though I was not

who he wanted to see. He was far more interested in the little girl hiding behind me.

"Hello, Evelyn," he said in a gentle voice. "Do you remember me? I'm your Papa."

She set her face firmly in a frown.

"I'm sorry I've been gone so long," he said. "Will you come and say hello to me? Well, that's all right. We'll try again in a little while."

Evelyn, grasping my skirt, ducked her face away. It would not be long, however, before she climbed into his lap to hear his stories or get her bedtime hugs.

For now, however, the Chief let shy Evelyn hide, and sank into his usual chair at the head of the table. He stared in disbelief around him. "What in the world has happened here?"

"I told you it was bad," Erlinda said, taking the chair beside his. She shot a hard look at the Bagobo men who stood awkwardly nearby. "Your tribesman will need to explain to you the failures of the past three years."

"And your mother?" Chief Doming asked.

Erlinda grimaced. "Still in Calinan, with *him*. I thought she might return when she heard of your release, but..."

The Chief shook his head with weariness. "Tomorrow, tomorrow. For tonight, let's just enjoy each other's company. Sit down, everyone."

He meant his children, and the two Bagobo men. They did sit. I helped the reluctant Evelyn into a chair. The meal on the table was paltry compared to what used to be served there. I doubted there was enough for everyone. And there was nothing else in the kitchen; I had put everything we had out for the Chief's return.

Once I'd seated Evelyn, I naturally turned to begin serving food to everyone. My nights of family meals were over, I supposed. The pretending was done. As poor as those meals had been, I realized I had cherished them.

Except Chief Doming did something that surprised me. As I reached for the first dish, he said, "Diamond, do we have you to thank for the meal?"

Thank me? My movements faltered. "Yes, Chief," I said. "I am sorry there isn't more."

"There will be more, soon," he said. "I'll set things right again. You may as well join us." He saw my confusion. "Have a seat, girl. Come on. Evelyn will be happier if you stay."

"We all will," said Dodong. So in a bit of a daze, I took an empty chair, and had my first meal with Chief Doming.

It took weeks for the Chief to get his estate running again. He went into his office for long hours at a time, day after day. Sometimes Erlinda came to help him. Bagobo people came and went. These were not "guests" of the house; the Chief never asked that they be served drinks or food. I suspected many of them arrived to find themselves seriously reprimanded for their behavior while the Chief had been away.

At the end of their meetings with the Chief, many would go slinking away like scolded children. Following a long closed-door meeting, a couple emerged, and as they left, I heard the wife telling her husband, "I *told* you! I said that the Chief would learn about your laziness and he certainly did!" The husband grumbled but would not meet her eyes.

Stories of Chief Doming's high temper were true, and now everyone knew he had served time for murdering those who had disobeyed him. People came to us anxiously, bringing their overdue rents or promises that crops and dividends would soon be back in order.

Slowly things became better. There was money again. Dodong, Orlando, and I went to the market to purchase staples the house needed badly, and it was a tremendous relief to see the pantry shelves filling once more. Now when I prepared meals, they were large enough, and had seasonings we'd been missing for some time.

I was allowed to continue having evening meals with the family. Despite the difficulties he faced, the Chief tried for the sake of his children to be cheerful when they were together.

Every other day or so, a new worker appeared in the yard. A new cook was hired, and I no longer had to prepare meals. Then a housekeeper came, and a maid to assist her, so the laundry and cleaning were taken out of my hands. Then a clerk came for Chief Doming's office. The trees and plants in the gardens behind the house were tended and began blooming once more. The house took on its old shine, as floors were once more polished, windows washed, bedrooms aired out.

One day, Chief Doming summoned me to his office. I saw many people leaving this room with frightened faces recently.

I thought about the past few years, the things I had done... his children, working in the yard! Allowing Dodong to sell the furniture, the curtains. Oh my goodness, the liberties I had taken! I thought of a thousand things the Chief could be angry about.

But when I entered his office, he smiled at me. When Chief Doming smiled, I could still see the handsome man he had been before. Could it be that I was not in trouble after all? When he spoke to me, his tone was different – this was the tone he usually reserved for his wife and children. It was affectionate.

"Most of our servants left while I was gone," said the Chief. "Why did you stay, Diamond?"

"I am very happy here, sir," I said. This was my standard answer; the one I always gave for fear of being sent away. I would have said this no matter what.

"You may sit down." He motioned to one of the chairs before his desk. I sat. Now the Chief and I looked at each other over stacks of paperwork still needing to be done. I could not hold his gaze for more than a second at a time.

"I have been speaking to Dodong," he told me. "It seems that, without you, my children would have suffered terribly. Dodong says that you kept them fed, and clothed, and even happy together. How did you manage that, here with nothing?"

I truly wished I was good with words, or brave enough to speak freely. Saying aloud what my heart felt remained difficult for me. I never could have explained my belief that God had a special plan for me, or my desperate love for the family I had here. But I could safely and honestly compliment his children. “Sir, it is my honor to care for the Apostol children. They are clever, and good, and never complained or misbehaved even though they missed you very much.”

The Chief nodded as I haltingly spoke. Then he said, “You’re a grown woman now, aren’t you?”

I actually had no idea. I was about eighteen. What would being a grown woman mean? It was strange, but I seldom thought about myself in the same terms as other people. I was a Japon; I didn’t even know if I was allowed to age like a normal girl.

The Chief didn’t expect me to respond. He said, “I’m not hiring a new nanny. You do the job better than anyone I could possibly hire, and the children adore you. Have the maids move your things into the nanny’s room, next to the nursery. We’ll need you there when Adela returns with Sarah. There may be more babies yet.”

I was nonplussed. Move my things? I had no things.

The Chief said, “There are very few people who did not abandon me and my family while I was gone. You deserve my gratitude. And you have it.”

His gratitude was welcome enough, but remaining in the children’s lives mattered more. I felt as if I’d been handed a gift. To me, the promotion to nanny was a reward from God for fulfilling my purpose.

Little did I know what my devotion to the Apostol family had in store for me.

## CHAPTER TWELVE

# THE NEW MISTRESS OF HOUSE APOSTOL

As time passed, the Apostol estate regained its previous importance. Chief Doming worked hard to put things right again. It was a lot of work, because Erlinda was starting her own family now and had less time to help him. The household was never quite as busy or exciting as it had been in the days of Adela, but tribal meetings resumed, and the Chief was once more in charge.

Several months after returning, the Chief ordered three of his men to go to the town of Calinan to find Lady Adela and baby Sarah. He hoped the refurbished house and improved finances would meet with Lady Adela's approval and she might come home. But when the men returned they came only with Sarah.

"Lady Adela will not return," they informed the Chief.

“She fears you will kill her. She sends your daughter now to appease you, and begs you to leave her in peace from now on.”

I feared that the Chief would fly into a rage, or go after Lady Adela himself. Instead, he withdrew into a pensive silence for a few days, brooding over his desk.

He seemed to come to a decision then, announcing to his children, “Your mother has abandoned us. Do not speak with her, write her letters, or try to see her. If she tries to contact you, or asks for money or favors, refuse, and tell me right away. She is no longer part of our family.”

This was hard news for the children, who had all harbored some hope that their father’s return would lead to their mother’s return as well. After so many disappointments, they bore this new development with strength. That was the point at which Dodong’s anger cemented, and he would never again have a close relationship with Lady Adela. Orlando tended to follow his elder brother in that manner. Rachel and Rodolfo clung to me a bit harder for a while, and I let them. As for Evelyn, she was so delighted to have Sarah returned that she hardly seemed to care that her mother would not be back, too.

Naturally, we were all delighted to have Sarah with us once more, though she required extra care and attention during the adjustment to a life without her mother. With the love of her father, siblings, and me, Sarah sprung back; she was a vivacious, courageous little thing who was always laughing. She brought such liveliness to the household.

At family dinners, I watched the Chief closely, if discreetly. My purpose was to ensure that I remained important and useful. Being such a careful observer, I learned much about the Chief as he interacted with his children, for he was coming to know them all over again. Each time he discovered something new about one of them, I watched his eyes fill with both pride and sadness. How terrible it must have been, to miss three entire years of their lives. For the first time, I began to see Chief Doming as a real person rather than an intimidating head of the house.

A few times at dinner, I even dared speak without being spoken to first. "Rodolfo had a big success at school today," I said once, because Rodolfo was not one to announce it for himself. The Chief turned bright, expectant eyes to his son and asked for the story.

To my astonishment, I also discovered that the new housekeeper and maids would take orders from me—orders I never meant to give. One morning when they were nearby, I said, mostly to myself, "The nursery is a mess and needs cleaning." When I went upstairs to take care of it, the job was already finished. The maid asked, a bit archly, if I was pleased with her work. I was too perplexed to answer, which she took to mean I was unhappy.

"What have I forgotten?" she wanted to know.

"It is fine, thank you," I said quickly. The maid left. There I stood for several long moments, until I pieced together the situation. When I understood I had something like "authority" around the household, I grew careful about things I said. I feared making trouble, or making myself disliked. I did not know how others might feel about taking orders from a Japon of low social status. All I knew for certain was that if I did not have the Apostol home, I had nowhere to go.

I was secretly pleased to learn that the leaders of the Bagobo tribe were encouraging the Chief to remarry. The idea seemed to come up at one of their council meetings, because the Chief mentioned it at the dinner table that night. Chief Doming spoke to his children, saying, "You all should know. The council thinks it is a good idea for me to marry again, to give you a new mother."

All activity stopped. The various Apostol children exchanged nervous glances. Sarah sat on my lap as I fed her, unaware that her siblings were upset. There were several moments of silence.

Dodong was the first one brave enough to speak. "Who do they want you to marry, Papa?"

"They are...discussing the matter," said Doming noncommittally.

"Someone from Magpet?" asked Orlando. "Someone we know?"

"I don't want a new mama," announced Evelyn. She was little enough that the Chief didn't become angry with her when she blurted out what the rest of them were thinking.

I knew the children were upset by this, but it was promising news to me. A new wife would certainly mean more children on the way, and if I continued to work hard and do my very best, I might keep my position for many years. *What if the new mistress dislikes me? What if she does not want a Japon caring for her children?* No, no—I pushed those thoughts aside. I had Doming's gratitude, and I hoped that would be enough to secure my place in the household.

When Chief Doming called me to his office again just a few days later, I assumed it was to tell me about the woman who would soon come to live with us, and what would be expected of me. I went with my hopes high. In his office, one of the elders of the Bagobo tribe stood with the Chief behind his desk.

"Please sit down, Diamond," said Chief Doming. He looked flustered. A pang of worry struck me. Could it be that I had misunderstood? That the new wife had her own nanny, or hated Japons? I did not wish to sit down. In fact I wanted to run away, so as not to hear whatever news had Chief Doming looking so uncomfortable. I slipped into a chair, folding my hands in my lap so they did not tremble.

The Bagobo elder was a man I had seen in the house often, but never before had he addressed me directly. Now he spoke with a certain amount of deference that I found just as alarming as a scolding. This was the way people acted when something was about to change.

He told me, "Diamon, we know you have been a mother to the Chief's children for many years now. And you are a strong, healthy girl, aren't you? The Council believes you are a good choice to become wife to the Chief."

I believed that I'd misheard him. The men looked at me expectantly, and I gave my head a quick little shake. "I don't understand."

The elder said, "You will marry Chief Doming. You're a very lucky girl."

Eternity ticked by as I looked at the Chief in disbelief. To my eyes, he looked nearly as old as the elder tribesman. For the first time ever, Chief Doming had trouble holding my gaze. He held a drink in one hand and swirled it nervously as he explained,"It is for the children, Diamond. Lady Adela's abandonment was crushing. They rely on you now to care for them."

But I was already doing that, and everything was fine exactly as it was! The idea of marriage to anyone had scarcely entered my mind. Who would want me? Now these two old men suggested I marry the Chief of the Bagobo tribe! My head could not take it all in.

"You are...teasing me," I muttered then, but even as I said, it I leaned forward, my muscles tensing, preparing to flee.

"This will be an honor for you," said the elder with patience. "Don't you see that? To be the mistress of this fine house is a respected position. You would not need to work, ever again. You can't possibly refuse such a privilege."

"No, no, no," I heard myself say distantly, scrambling from the chair and rushing to the door. I fumbled with it, unable to make it work. I heard their voices behind me.

The elder was actually laughing. "Silly child, come back here, and sit down."

"Let her go," said Chief Doming. "She's a shy girl. It's a lot to take in."

At last, I flung the door wide and skidded into the front hall. Then I ran for my room. Halfway up the staircase, I realized I had left a meeting without permission, disobeyed instructions, and refused to do what I was told. I could be banished. I could be punished. Once in my room I began to pace, frantically, biting at my fingernails.

*Mistress of this fine house!* Was I to marry a man more than twice my age? I was barely older than Erlinda. Plus this was Chief Doming. No matter how many dinners we had shared as a family since his return, I suddenly could not think of him as anything other than the Chief of the Bagobo tribe.

Time passed; I don't know how much. There came a gentle knocking on my door. Fear clenched my throat as I went to answer. I don't know who I expected, but to my relief, most of the Apostol children stood before me: Dodong, Orlando, Rodolfo, and Rachel.

"Where are the little ones?" I asked in alarm, suddenly remembering it was my job to watch them.

Dodong told me, "They are in the kitchen with the cook. It's all right." The four of them shuffled in and stood before me. Dodong looked at his siblings, each of whom gave him a nod, and then he turned back to me. "Diamond, we would be happy to have you as our new mother. You are already a mother to us and have been for years. If you marry our father, we won't need to pretend anymore."

Orlando agreed, adding, "If you don't, Papa might marry someone we don't like."

"She might be cruel or send us away," Rachel worried.

"We want you, not anyone else," Rodolfo finished.

I couldn't believe this was happening. All I knew was that the children of my heart were asking something of me. How could I refuse them? I heard a noise from the doorway and looked up in alarm. Doming stood there. If he had not seemed a bit uncertain himself, I might yet have balked at the idea. Thankfully, he understood my shock and fear.

I admitted, “Chief, I don’t know what to do.”

He chuckled softly. “I suppose that, first, you must call me Doming.”

CHAPTER THIRTEEN

# NEW LADY, NEW LIFE

For the second time in my life, my world turned upside down. This time, though, instead of losing my family and identity, I gained both things, almost overnight. With a ceremony and a few words, I was turned from Diamond the Japon into Mrs. Apostol, and I was now the stepmother of seven children—the oldest two of whom were practically my own age.

The younger children sometimes called me "Mama" or "Mama Diamond." Dodong was a bit too old for "Mama," but he called me "Diamond" and treated me with enthusiastic respect and affection. The children were the easy part. They were the anchors that kept me steady when everything else was bewildering. Little changed between us. Or, I suppose I should say, little changed between me and the younger six.

Erlinda did not know what to make of my becoming

Mrs. Apostol. She was confused by the union. While she understood that the Bagobo tribe had sanctioned the marriage and that her siblings were pleased about it, I'm sure she worried that her father had been saddled with a burden or an embarrassment when he was "forced" to marry me. I am certain she took him aside more than once and seriously questioned him to ensure that all was well. I wonder if she suspected me of subterfuge and seduction—as if I even knew what those things meant. Toward me, she was cool but civil. I knew that she and I would never be close like I was with her brothers and sisters.

My change in status was far harder to cope with than any suspicions from Erlinda—no matter how many servants worked in the house or the yard, no matter how polite the Bagobo chiefs were to me, no matter how Doming and the children reminded me of my position, no matter if no person in the town of Magpet dared to shout names at me ever again. Inside, I still saw myself as that lost child, at the mercy of fate. At any moment, everything might change again, and the only way I could protect myself was by being small, quiet, unnoticeable. I must not make trouble. I must obey.

I don't mean to sound as if my life was a misery. Far from it. In so many ways, I had everything I had ever longed for, and more than I'd dared to hope I might ever have. I simply didn't know what to do with it all.

The large house was now mine to walk about in as I pleased. I moved into Adela's suite of rooms, some of which were shared with Doming. How odd it must have seemed to the servants of the house—that in a matter of a couple of years, I had gone from servant to nanny to lady of the house.

Well, it certainly felt odd to me. For a long time, I occupied no more than a little corner of the great bedroom. Though I had helped clean these rooms and changed the linens many times, the sheer size of the space suddenly staggered me. I felt almost agoraphobic trying to navigate from the master bedroom to the children's room to the private parlor, which had a fancy recliner and sofas! It was months before I finally felt comfortable enough to put my things in the wardrobe. It was months before I had enough things to put there.

I no longer needed to work. The sudden lack of chores left me reeling. I didn't know what to do with myself. It took me weeks to understand that I was bored. Soon I found tasks for myself to do around the house, snatching chores right out from under the servants. Rather than ordering someone to clean, fetch, or carry, I often just did it myself.

At first the housekeeper, maids, and cook tried gently to dissuade me from this.

"Good heavens, Diamon," one might say. "It's my job to mend the children's clothing. Are you unhappy with my work?"

Or "Diamon, the Chief will have my head if he sees you outside gathering vegetables!"

I assured them as best I could. "Your work is excellent. Please, I like to do these things. I enjoy it."

They could not exactly order me to stop. And when Doming caught me doing things that he called "servants' work," rather than becoming angry, he just found it funny. "Diamond, can't you ever be still and stop working?" he teased. "We should put you in charge of the farms; they'd get twice as much done."

But of course he could not put me in charge of anything. I was illiterate, and no farmhands or tenants would ever take orders from me, should I even grow brave enough to give them. I stayed in the Apostol house—my house—most of the time, content to tend to the clockwork of this little universe I could call my own.

I had the notion that "ladies" were allowed, even expected, to do certain things: shop, write letters, dine, read magazines, dress in fancy clothes, sleep late, tell servants what to do, and—to my bafflement—*entertain*. The life of a lady was there before me, but I didn't want it, even if I *had* understood how to embrace it. Shy I may have been, and uneducated, and unsophisticated, but I had a streak of steely stubbornness that had carried me through my whole life. I made it quietly clear from the start that I would not be cajoled or bullied into remaking myself, as if I might replace Adela. Not only was it impossible, but the efforts would have infuriated me.

So I was the "reclusive" mistress of the house. People understood. As it happened, life in Magpet went on exactly as it had before I married Doming, and that was quite a relief. I had enough adjustments to make without expectations from the town or tribe.

But what of Doming himself? And what of my suddenly being a wife, thrust into a marriage to a man more than twice my age? Not to mention, a man of considerable experience and high temper, holding more power than anyone else in Magpet. I admit that I had little idea of what to expect or what I was meant to do. I certainly had no mother or older woman to advise me, and no role models to imitate.

Luckily, Doming seemed as uncertain as I felt in the beginning. Seeing me as something other than a servant was hard for him. Not that he was disrespectful, but aside from the children, we had little to talk about. Besides, I was far too intimidated to try getting to know him. I did what I had always done before: watch carefully, listen intensely, glean all the information I could get without ever drawing attention.

I suppose someone observing us might have thought it comical. For some time, we tiptoed around each other, exchanging nervous niceties like two strangers forced to travel together for convenience. When he was in the family suite, I almost tripped over myself to stay out of his way. I did not know if I was permitted to use certain things. I asked permission before picking up a hairbrush or a cake of soap. Doming usually found this amusing and would say, "Silly girl, you don't have to ask. These things are yours now. Use them. I don't care!"

One day he walked into the bedroom, and I scurried quickly to a chair, tucking my legs up under me. He grew annoyed. "Stop jumping away from me like a rabbit!"

"I don't want to be a bother," I confessed. "Don't want to be in the way."

He seemed to realize he'd snapped at me. He calmed his tone and said, "But Diamond, you are my wife now. You are not in the way. I like to see you. You're pretty to look at, and pleasant to speak with, and my children love you."

Compliments—they were always difficult for me. My cheeks flamed. I clasped my knees and looked away.

Doming crept closer, pretending slyness. "Perhaps I am in your way. Ugly old Doming, tromping around, making a ruckus and messing up the room."

I couldn't help but laugh, covering my face with my hands.

"Grrrrr!" he roared, slouching through the room. I'd seen him chase his children this way, pretending to be a gorilla. He'd have them laughing and racing around until they were breathless.

"You are not ugly," I dared to tell him.

He burst into laughter, loud enough to startle me. "But old, right? And very much in the way!"

Suddenly gorilla-Doming lunged at me and I scampered out of reach—not exactly in fear, though. In a moment he was chasing me around the room. If I had truly been frightened, I might have run out the door. Instead, I stayed within, and though I never quite dared to make much noise, my sides were soon aching with laughter. When he caught me—or did I let myself be caught?—he gave me a quick kiss on the forehead. "Now, no more ducking away. You make me feel like a brute."

Our relationship took time, and Doming generously allowed me the time I needed to adjust. I gave him time, too, my sharp intuition guiding me. We began edging through stages of our relationship: moving past being an employer and his servant, to a state that mimicked a father with a daughter he did not know well, as I learned to trust him. But of course we were a married couple, and the relationship evolved as we learned how to be together in quiet moments alone.

You see, when I was just a small child, Doming rescued me and gave me the only safe home I'd ever had. He was my savior in so many ways. My gratitude for that was boundless, such a deep-rooted part of me that I recognized it like my own hands or face. And I had done something for him in return, caring for his children when no one else would do so.

Our mutual respect made a solid bond between us that grew into love. I don't know precisely when it happened, but happen it did. And so I loved Doming Apostol as my husband, and through that, understood what it meant to be his wife.

Our first baby, a beautiful girl we named Virgie, was born in 1960. When I held her, and introduced her to her older brothers and sisters, I thought, *If this was God's plan for me all along, then I am more than happy to accept it.*

CHAPTER FOURTEEN

# A FAMILY TOGETHER

Over the next decade, more children were born to me and Doming, adding to our busy, noisy, happy home. After our little Virgie came Mildred in 1962, Grace in 1964, and Gary in 1967. Just when I believed my heart could not hold any more love, a new baby would prove me wrong. Children make our hearts bigger, and there is plenty of room.

Many things can be said about Doming Apostol, it is true, but no one could ever doubt he was a loving father who adored all his children.

He made time for every child: to admire Erlinda's business savvy and her growing family, to bicker with Dodong but smile in admiration at the boy's talent and determination, to brag about what fine men Orlando and Rodolfo were becoming, to show patience and chivalry to shy Rachel, to help Evelyn and Sarah adjust to life without their birth mother and begin growing up. Then after we were married, I watched him with our babies, each of whom he cuddled and fussed over, delighting in their daily discoveries. He was a proud papa, ready to show off his brilliant sons and daughters to the tribesmen.

Through those years, my children were always my priority above anything else. My little ones had nannies, because it was only proper that children of the Apostol household should. Yet I never gave over their care entirely to anyone else. I had no "ladylike" aversion to diapers, messy meals, or nighttime cries. I was usually at their side before a nanny could reach them, to soothe away nightmares or clean up spills, gather them up into big hugs and promise that all was well—and Doming was right there beside me.

All my children were precious. I looked to them to see myself, because without them I was lost. It was through Doming and Adela's children that I learned to love and value myself. Then I strove to be a steady, loving influence to make up for what they had lost. When my own babies came, I fiercely determined that they, too, should never be frightened, or hungry, or lonely. I wanted them to know each day how cherished they were.

Doming was a good papa instinctively because it brought him joy and pride. I tried to be a good mother because of joy and pride, too, but also because I knew what it was to be alone, and without love.

In 1965, the Philippines came under the rule of Ferdinand Marcos, and the politics of the country changed dramatically. We were far from Manila, though. The island of Mindanao didn't figure much into world politics. And I paid little attention to such things.

More important to me was that Virgie was old enough to start school soon. As a parent, it was so strange to see my first child—who was surely just a baby only months before!—walk off toward school alongside Evelyn and Sarah, with her little book bag gripped in one hand, her head held high. The pathway led through the orchard behind the house.

"Please look out for Virgie," I pleaded to the girls as they headed away.

Evelyn assured me, "We will take good care of her, Mama Diamond."

"Yes, we promise!" Sarah assured me. She held Virgie's hand as they walked away. The school was nearby. I could see it from the yard, but it suddenly seemed like it was too far away.

"Mildred will be next," Doming said when he saw my mixed emotions.

"Oh no! Not for another year or two."

"It will come before you know it!" he teased. Then he put his arm around me for a tight squeeze. "I've done this many times. It will be all right. Virgie will be the smartest in her class and make you prouder than ever."

He was right, of course.

Some days meant park excursions, when the maids would make picnic baskets and we all headed out for a day playing in the hot sunshine. Bodyguards accompanied us everywhere we went. Glad for their presence, I nevertheless wondered why we needed them. Doming told me very little about his business.

When I asked about the bodyguards, he said, "I do everything I can to keep my family safe." He didn't want to worry me, I'm sure, but he forgot what a good observer I could be. I deduced the truth: he feared the children might be kidnapped and held for ransom. I was therefore only too happy to enforce the house rules. The children were told to stay on the property except for school. With the enormous orchard, there was plenty of room for them to play.

During the children's summer breaks, Doming often took us to Davao for vacations. Though he could be frugal in some ways, he was a big spender on those trips. We stayed in the home of some friends of his; they had a beautiful place large enough to accommodate all of us.

The first time we went, I worried that Davao would overwhelm or frighten me. I'd never been to the city. I only remembered one cranky nanny, years ago, who had come from this place and had told me such terrible stories. She'd convinced me that Davao was even dangerous for Japons. "They *hate* Japons in Davao," she had said more than once.

Regardless of what she'd said, my experience was quite different. Davao was bright and busy, and no one was ever even rude to me. While in the city, we attended parties and visited relatives, shopped in the many stores, and ate at restaurants. The activity and noise fascinated me. The people we visited were unfailingly kind and accepting of me. I came to love these trips, each one an adventure in new experiences. Doming liked to treat me to new things because I was as excited as the children, maybe more so.

I still vividly remembered a time when I had nothing and no one, so I was grateful for everything good that came my way. I tried to show my children how to be grateful as well. "Isn't it wonderful to have each other and all these nice things?" I asked. "We must always recognize how lucky we are." And my husband made each trip unforgettable. He wanted to show us all a good time, and so he did.

Magpet had small fashion retailers and groceries, but nothing like Davao. Doming had an extravagant habit of inviting Davao retailers to visit our home once or twice each year. They came up the dusty road with a truckload of treasures: clothes, shoes, handbags, fabrics, makeup, toys, and a dazzling variety of imported goods—all of it for the Apostol household only. For that day, our downstairs hall became like a busy boutique as boxes piled up and the children exclaimed over the contents. Doming bought everything on the truck and made certain that everyone, including the servants, got something new. The children considered it a second Christmas.

Surrounded by all this love, every day felt like Christmas to me.

I had the guilty pleasure of a favorite radio program. On weekday afternoons I took half an hour all for myself to listen to *Flor de Luna*. The story was similar to the fairy tale of Cinderella. Maria *Flor de Luna*, the young heroine, suffered when her widowed father remarried. While he was away, the stepmother and stepsisters mistreated her. Of course, the happy conclusion was when the father came back home, the wicked stepmother and stepsister were punished, and the girl lived happily ever after. I loved the idea of it, identifying with the girl who waited for her loving parent's return.

When the radio show turned into a movie, it was a big hit in the neighboring town. We had no movie house in Magpet, so I begged Doming to allow me to travel to the next town to see the film. It took days, but he finally let me and the children go to the movie, accompanied by the usual set of bodyguards. The movie house was crowded, but I didn't mind. I enjoyed the film so much that for weeks afterward I talked about it with Virgie and Mildred.

"Isn't it wonderful to think of such happy endings?" I asked them.

Mostly I let Doming dictate how the household and family were run. This was for many reasons. I was not assertive, not even in my new position as Mrs. Apostol. A lifetime of subservience was still ingrained in me, along with that long-trained habit of quiet watchfulness that had always served me well. I was uncomfortable about making demands. Besides, most of the time, I agreed with whatever Doming thought was best. I only occasionally put a gentle hand on his shoulder, to suggest that he calm down and think before making a rash decision.

There was one time, however, when I requested a favor,

and stood my ground.

For years I had been friends with a lovely, hardworking, young woman called Celing. Her family settled in Magpet in the early 1960s. She and her husband had five children. Like most women in Magpet, Celing was a housewife who stayed home to raise the family while her husband was the breadwinner. I remember that her husband went from town to town looking for a job until finally he found one in a nearby logging company.

Logging had its hazards, though, and a tragic accident took Celing's husband from her. She was left with five children to raise on her own, with no life insurance or stipend from the logging company. They were suddenly destitute. Celing and I spoke about everything, and I knew what a struggle it was for her to keep her children fed. Her husband's family was affluent, but to my horror, extending Celing the help she needed was not a priority to them. I could never understand how families could turn their backs on one another this way. Troubles like that always made me think of what I would give to have known my own parents. It baffled me that families could dismiss each other so casually.

Nevertheless, when I became Mrs. Apostol, there was something I could do for Celing.

I spoke to Doming over the breakfast table, after the children had scattered to get ready for school. I said, "I would like to hire a full-time laundry maid."

He was unaccustomed to me asking for anything, and looked up in surprise. "Is something wrong with the laundry? Don't the maids do a good job?"

"The maids are busy with other chores," I said. "We need someone for the laundry full-time. Do you know how much laundry children can make? Baskets full every day! There are always dirty clothes to clean. My friend Celing is a very experienced laundress. You should hire her. She needs a job, and we need the help."

I think Doming could count on one hand the times when I had spoken that many sentences in a row. He knew I was serious. He thought for a moment, then said, "No, no...we have plenty of fulltime help. If you think the laundry isn't being done well enough, say something to the housekeeper." Then, in a gentler tone, he added, "Or I will talk to her, if it makes you nervous to say something."

He started to look back at his newspaper, but I interrupted him. "No, I want you to hire Celing."

This astonished my husband. "Oh, really?"

I pressed my hands together to keep them steady. I did not fear Doming, but I was never at ease with asserting myself. "Her husband has died. He was their only provider. She has nothing and five children to raise. She is my friend, Doming. She is too proud to take charity. Imagine how you would feel, if I were left alone to care for our children with no help from anyone."

Doming's eyebrows raised; either the thought had never crossed his mind, or it seemed impossible to him.

I had his attention, so I continued quickly. "Celing will work hard and do a good job, and we have so much here... surely we can afford to pay a laundress." I paused and then added, "Please, as a favor to your wife. You will not regret it."

I held his gaze as he thought. He was both surprised and a bit proud of me, for finally speaking out about something I wanted. Many times, he chided me, if gently, about my reticence to speak or make my wishes known.

He folded his newspaper. "Very well then. We will hire your friend Celing as our laundress. Shall I tell the housekeeper, or will you?"

I was thrilled. "I will tell her! Yes! Thank you, Doming!"

So Celing was hired, and as I had promised, she worked very hard as a laundress for our household. But I insisted that she be allowed each day to go home and care for her children. As often as I could, I sent her home with goodies from the pantry. Celing would not accept charity for herself, but she never argued when I offered treats for her little ones. It made my heart swell with happiness to be able to help her. I suddenly had so much wonderful and unexpected good fortune in my life that I was delighted to help someone in need.

All the while, we remained good friends, seeing each other to talk every day. As shy as I was, it was hard for me to make close friendships, so I cherished what Celing and I shared.

After a few more years, Celing remarried. Her new husband was glad to provide for her and all of her children. This was wonderful news for Celing, and of course, I was happy for her. However, her new husband relocated the family, which broke my heart. Saying goodbye to my dear friend was painfully difficult. For many weeks after she and her family moved away, I cried during my prayers, asking God to protect Celing and keep her safe, and to help heal my heart from the pain of losing another friend.

In the summers, the weather could be miserably hot in Magpet during the daytime, but the nights were pleasant. Going to bed as early as 8 pm was quite normal. The children gathered in the family room on the second floor, where the servants gave them warm milk to help them sleep better. Every so often, I remembered miserable nights as a child, sleeping on the ground, tormented by insects, and felt so thankful that my children never had to endure that.

One night after I kissed each one of them and then sent them to their papa for his good nights, Doming and I proudly smiled at each other.

"What beautiful children," Doming said, loudly enough that they could hear him. He waved as the nanny shuffled them off to bed.

"They have a very handsome papa," I said. "He is also clever and very generous."

"Tell me more about this wonderful papa," joked Doming. But there was a strange light in his eyes that night. I could tell something was bothering him.

"What's wrong?"

"Wrong? Oh, nothing much...or perhaps something. Nights like this make me wonder about Simplicio."

He meant his son, the child he'd had with his third-cousin Inday, many years ago. The rumors of the staff had alerted me when I was just a child that Doming had left mother and son behind when he was forced to escape Inday's angry father in Cebu. But Doming dispelled me of the idea that Inday had killed herself. "That's just servants' gossip," he said. "No, Inday was too strong to do something like that. And her family would not throw her out. I just wonder sometimes, what became of my son."

He knew little else, however. Contact had been severed.

"You could write a letter," I said. "Surely after all this time, they cannot still be angry with you."

"I don't know. I don't care what Inday's family says, but Simplicio might have grown up hating me."

"If that is true, it's only because he does not know you."

"You're too kind to me, Diamond."

"I know you are a wonderful father," I insisted. "Someday you must seek out Simplicio. Let him know that you think of him often."

"Perhaps I will," said Doming, thoughtfully.

But for now, he waited.

CHAPTER FIFTEEN

# NIGHT OF THE BLADES

I am sad to say that my happiness and good fortune took a dark turn. It happened slowly and subtly at the beginning, so for a time I only thought this was one of those difficult patches that many marriages face. By the time I recognized how much danger I was in, it was almost too late.

I do not remember exactly the first time Doming struck me. He was so much older than me, and I found it difficult to understand the changes he experienced. But in the late 1960s, his temper, always unpredictable, grew worse. I could no longer calm him with a gentle touch or a soft suggestion. Anytime I tried to divert his mood, things became worse.

When his tenants or tribesmen angered him, he ranted and shouted. If I was in the way, even in the room, I found myself being pushed or smacked. First it was just the rough actions of an irritated man, thrusting me aside or smacking my hand if I touched something he was using. Then it grew into real blows that bruised my skin. Then it became worse still—punches and kicks that struck me while I cowered on the floor.

As he aged, Doming became ever more jealous. He said crazy things, like accusing me of looking for a younger man out in Magpet. Maybe he feared I would do as Adela had done, and leave him for another man. This was preposterous. I would never have dreamed of such a thing, first of all. Moreover, I rarely left the house, being far happier to stay secluded and away from the town that had few good memories for me.

But if I tried to convince Doming of this, it only made him angrier. "Don't argue with me!" he would shout, shaking me roughly. "I know what's happening in my town. I know what's happening in my home! I see everything!"

A distant cousin of the family, a young man of about thirty, came to live with us for a time. This was not unusual; whenever relatives came from Cebu, they stayed at the Apostol house, and Victor was no different. Victor always treated me with great respect and called me "Auntie Diamond." He was good company and even helped around the house. Unfortunately, Doming's thinking had grown so paranoid and mistrustful that he began believing Victor and I were having an affair. He peered at us constantly, listening to any words we might exchange. There was nothing for Doming to discover, yet he seemed determined to find something to blame us for. Poor Victor soon realized that Doming was suspicious, and Victor knew better than to linger too near an angry, jealous Doming. Rather than tempt fate, he left Magpet and returned to Cebu.

What madness seized Doming sometimes, I do not know. And I was helpless to stop it, for many reasons. Deep inside, I believed I must endure whatever he did. He was my husband, yes. He was also Doming. A little voice inside of me was certain that if I displeased him, he could send me away from the only home I'd ever known and from my babies. I had nothing else but this, so if my husband chose to beat me, what could I do about it? I endured it and hoped he would change his mind, change his ways, and come to love and trust me again.

Enduring, though, was desperately difficult, especially since the children could see what was happening. More than once Evelyn intervened.

She stood between her father and me, wailing, "Papa, don't hit Mama Diamond! You're making her cry!" He told her to go to her room, but she stood her ground. She was as brave as a warrior. Only at the behest of his fearless daughter would Doming stop his tirades against me. He stormed away, slamming the door of his office, and Evelyn rushed to me, hugging me gently.

"He doesn't mean it, Mama Diamond," she told me. "Are you all right now?"

I tried not to show her how badly this hurt me. The pain of bruises wasn't even the worst of it. The pain of uncertainty and fear—those were far worse. I forced myself to smile and say, "I'm fine, Evelyn. Your papa just has a bad temper, but he would never hurt you."

“I know, but I don’t want him to hurt you, either,” said Evelyn.

For months this went on, and the situation became more frightening when in 1969 I discovered that I was expecting another child. I hoped that pregnancy would stop Doming from striking me, if only for the child’s sake. And it did, in a way—he no longer kicked or punched my body, only struck my face, and not so often as before. But now his rage turned to a new suspicion.

“Is the child even mine?” he accused. “Have you been with someone else?” And no matter how much I told him the truth, he would not believe it for long. For a few days he might be all right, then something would trigger his ire again and I would see his eyes turn glaring toward me, blaming me for some imaginary sin against him.

Then the day came when I could stand it no longer. Doming was in an especially foul mood. Issues bombarded him from the town, the lands, and the tribe. A dozen things were going wrong. As he prepared to leave home to handle these problems, I was unlucky enough to be in the way.

“I could kill these fools, you know. I suppose you’d be happy if I did,” he snarled at me. “If I went to prison again, you’d be free to carry on with your new man, wouldn’t you?”

I did not know how to answer this accusation. It was too much. I simply shook my head violently. I didn’t want any of that.

He gripped my shoulders. “No? No I shouldn’t kill these idiots? No, I shouldn’t go back to prison again? Why not? Things were better when I was behind bars in Manila. At least I didn't have to watch my wife sneak around behind my back!"

"Doming, please," I begged, worrying for the baby. "Everything will be all right. Just talk to the tenants and explain..."

"Don't give me orders in my own home!" he said, thrusting me away from him. "I've had enough of your lies and deception. If I manage to survive this day, I'll kill you myself tonight. You're not going to have another man's child and make a fool out of me."

Then he was gone, leaving me quaking.

I believed him. He'd gone mad and thought I was the cause of his troubles. So many terrifying ideas struck me now. Had he actually been forced to marry me against his wishes? Did I really make him this unhappy? Was I at fault for everything? Did he have a right to kill me if he wanted to?

It did not matter. That steely streak of stubbornness in me rose up to resist. I would not let Doming kill me. I might have only been a lower-class Japon underneath it all, but God had a purpose for me, and it was not to die at the hands of Doming Apostol for a crime I had never committed.

Before Doming returned, I instructed the nanny to see to the children. "I have an errand I must run," I told her. It was one of the few lies I'd ever told. I wanted to embrace each of the children individually and tell them how much I loved them, but I might start crying, and that behavior would seem strange. I couldn't alert anyone to what I was doing.

I had no wish to leave my children. I couldn't bear thinking about it, so I made myself think of nothing. Even as I snuck out into Magpet to hide in the shadows, I kept my thoughts blank and focused only on escape. Doming would never harm our children, and they would be well cared for in his home.

I took nothing with me, and had no money and nowhere to go, so my children would only be endangered if I tried to pull them alongside me. Better to vanish than be murdered in front of them! Better to have an absent mother and a loving father, than to have a dead mother and a father in prison, or worse, executed.

The roads from Magpet were rocky and unpaved. Little traffic came through on them, and those few vehicles moved slowly. No one dared to drive fast due to the rough conditions. Still, I could not afford to be seen, so I would have to make my way through the jungle.

Just as I had done when I was a child hiding from bullies, I huddled in a dark Magpet alley until the darkness was almost complete. Then I crept into the thick, wild forest that surrounded the town. I planned to make my way to the next town, Kidapawan, where I knew a Baptist minister lived. I still remembered my friend Brother Tim with deep affection, and I knew Brother Tim would have helped me out of this, had he been there. I could only hope that this other Baptist minister would be as kind as Brother Tim had once been.

With nothing but the clothes on my back, I hiked through the night, covering the fourteen miles to the next town through formidable terrain. The tree branches scratched at me. The ground tripped me. Soon my entire body ached. The cogon grass ripped at my skin. When I was a child, I learned to avoid this awful plant. Around Magpet they called it "bloody grass" or "blade grass," so sharp and coarse were its leaves. It could cut like a razor. In the darkness that night, I could not avoid it. My arms and legs grew numb from the vicious cuts. I was covered in my own blood, my shoes soggy with it. My face streamed with tears of fear, grief, and pain. I do not know how I continued. If not for that steely resolve within me, I'm certain I never would have made it through.

I came to a river with no bridge in sight. I surveyed it. I knew how to swim, if not expertly, and the water did not look very deep or rapid. So I took off my shoes and held them in my hands, then sloshed in, wincing as the cold water stung my slashed skin. The current pushed at me, but I walked the breadth of the river without much trouble. On the other side, I put my shoes back on. Soaking wet, I plunged back into the jungle.

I came to another river not long afterward and groaned with weariness. I was only beginning to feel dry again. The first river had been alright, and this one didn't look any bigger. Once again I removed my shoes and stepped into the water.

But the moonlight was no longer as bright, the moon having moved lower in the sky, and the darkness and my exhaustion misled me. I was up to my pregnant belly in water when my next step landed on a viciously jagged stone on the river bottom. I gasped in pain and tried to push away, only to have more stones strike my legs, knocking and scraping at my shins and ankles. My feet went out from under me, and the current snatched me up.

The darkness had concealed from me the terrible, rocky bottom of this river and the power of the current. I was dragged over painful jutting rocks, swallowing water and choking as I tried to right myself. Panic overtook me as I repeatedly failed to put my feet back on the river bottom. Stones struck me again and again, adding to my terror. When I realized I could no longer find the bottom at all, I came close to screaming for help before my head went underwater again. I did not scream—I was as afraid of discovery as I was of drowning—and the water filled my nose and mouth once more.

Suddenly my body struck a boulder big enough to grab onto, and so I did. The solidity of it allowed me to get my head above water, reorient myself, steel myself against the angry current, and catch my breath. I shook so violently that I felt sick, but made myself calm down. The rocks bruised me, but no bones were broken, and I had instinctively protected the baby. I thanked God for saving me, but at the same time, I cried with despair.

I could not go back, so I must forge ahead. The shore was a few meters away, and I thought I could make it if I kept my wits and moved slowly. I let go of the boulder and stepped with deliberation toward the shoreline. The effort it took to stand against the current was exhausting. The stones on the riverbed were sharp on my bare feet and grew more painful as I emerged from the water and lost buoyancy. My shoes were gone, swept away by the river. Finally, there I was, barefoot, half-drowned, and on the opposite side of a river I dared not cross again. For only a moment, I thought it might be easier to climb back into the river and let it take me.

But, no—my inner strength would not allow that thought to linger. Instead, I prayed that God would grant me endurance, and protect me and the baby I carried. That prayer became a repeated mantra as the hours dragged on. As it was, I fell into a sort of stupor, from exhaustion and pain, thirst and hunger, stumbling along through the vicious jungle as the sun eventually began to warm the sky.

After what seemed like an eternity, I blinked and found myself standing on the outskirts of Kidapawan. It was morning, and the townspeople were moving about, taking little notice of me. Unsteady, as if in a dream, I dragged my weary body toward the building with a cross on top. I pushed the door open and stumbled inside. For several moments I stood, blinking as my tired eyes adjusted to the shade.

Nearby stood a man—by his skin color, I could tell he must be the pastor—with his wife at his side. They stared at me in horror and dismay. My clothes were ruined, my hair matted, and every exposed inch of my skin was bruised, cut, and swollen. I must have looked like I'd been chased through the night by wild dogs, like a battered, bloody, jungle animal that had finally fallen accidentally into their church.

The wife spoke first, crying, "You poor child! What happened to you?"

"My name is Diamond Apostol," I said as I sank weakly onto the rough plank of a pew. "My husband says he is going to kill me, for something I did not do. Would you help me, please?"

CHAPTER SIXTEEN

# REGRET AND FORGIVENESS

Doming was furious when he realized I was gone, and not just to run an errand, as the tearful nanny assured him, but vanished completely from his home. For a time, it probably confirmed to him his every suspicion about me. I imagine he thought I had run away to be with my paramour.

The night of my escape, he gathered his bodyguards and went house to house in Magpet, searching for me. He pounded on doors and demanded entry, shouting that whoever sheltered me would be punished for doing so. He had the surrounding roads searched as well, but he never dreamed I would do something as crazy as traveling through the treacherous jungle.

Doming underestimated my determination and resilience. He didn't conceive that I could have made it to another town. He, like others, may have thought my shyness and quiet nature meant that I was weak. They were wrong.

It pains me terribly to say that my children were affected by my absence. Of course they were. I, too, knew the turmoil of losing a parent. And my little ones were well-known as the children of Doming. Rumors spread around the school, and the children were bombarded with questions. Teachers and students gossiped. Some were even bold enough to approach the children to ask for details. To ease their stress, Doming removed them from school for several days. Doming had donated the land for the school, so the principal was amenable when the children had to stay home. Trying to take their minds off their troubles, Doming sent them on distracting excursions, as if they were on a holiday.

Meanwhile, the rumors festered throughout the town of Magpet. Doming was not subtle as he'd pushed down doors to find me; everyone knew I was gone. It was not helpful for his reputation. Could a man who lost his own wife be a good chief? Had Doming lost his touch? Why did Diamond run away? What did he do to her? Why would she leave such a fortunate situation? Speculation ran wild. The tribe pressured Doming to fix this, though how he was meant to repair the damage, I do not know.

One might suppose, at this point, that Doming's fury would worsen, that he would now have a genuine cause to hate me instead of the wild stories in his imagination. If I had known what was happening, I might have feared even more for my life. Who knows what behavior the town of Magpet might have tolerated, if it meant Doming was putting his house in order? I was just a Japon. If he had killed me... no, it is useless to speculate.

Doming was not a bad man; I never thought him so. I thought he was a man with a devilish temper who had never been taught self-control. He was accustomed to being popular, respected, and unquestioningly in charge; the one time that had not happened, he had murdered three men. When things went wrong, he rebelled like a child might. But he was intelligent, too. He was able to learn from mistakes. My absence gave him time to think.

He knew, and the children knew, what had happened between us. I know that they defended me to him, as they longed for my return. Evelyn was never one to mince words. I am certain she told her father frankly that, "Mama Diamond left us because you hurt her and scared her."

"She never had anything to fear from me," Doming argued dully. But he knew this was not true.

My days at the parsonage were some of the strangest I had ever spent. My entire body hurt from the injuries I'd sustained in the jungle; I was exhausted, dehydrated, and nauseous—conditions made even more difficult by my pregnancy—and it took me some days to recuperate. When not deep in healing slumber, I would sometimes sit in the hard pews of the church looking at the cross on the wall, trying to find meaning in this awful situation.

As I whispered a prayer to my Heavenly Father, tears streamed down my face. I implored God for my baby's health and safety. I prayed that I would never be separated from my little one. This tiny life growing within me was all I had left, and I was determined to protect it at all costs.

I had never been on my own; now, I faced a life of near solitude. I felt more lost than ever. The pastor and his wife discussed possibilities with me, and we talked about sending me to the city, someplace where Doming couldn't find me. There, I could raise the baby in peace.

The idea of going to another place filled me with wonder and dread. That was impossible, wasn't it? I knew nothing except housekeeping and childrearing. Was I meant to work somewhere, to earn an income, while trying to care for an infant? But what other option did I have?

Stillness never sat well with me. I wasn't accustomed to it. If I wasn't worrying about my own uncertain future, I grieved the loss of my children. I often wept with loneliness for them, recalling their voices, their laughter, the smell of their skin. As soon as I was able to move about with less pain, I drove the minister's wife crazy, as I found ever more chores to keep myself busy. The parsonage had never been so clean and tidy.

My need for activity overcame thoughts of my own safety, and one day I went out to the water pump to wash clothes. That was where I was seen, and word got back to Doming that I was at the Baptist parsonage in Kidapawan.

The day after I was sighted, I was polishing pews in the church—for the second time, and how they gleamed! I was in a frantic state, for the very next day, a car was coming to take me to Davao, then beyond, to the home of a distant relation where it would be impossible for Doming to find me. Utterly terrified at this vast unknown future, I scrubbed and polished until my arms ached.

Suddenly the pastor was beside me, looking deeply concerned. "Diamond, your family is outside. Your husband. He is here."

I straightened, the rag falling from my hand, my heart pounding.

"Doming has brought your children. He begged me to let the children see you." The pastor shook his head. "I wouldn't let them in here because it must be your choice. The door is locked right now and you are safe. But if you want to go out, I'll stay nearby so he can't hurt you."

I raced for the door. At that moment, I thought of nothing except seeing my babies again. The very idea that they were just outside the church doors drove all other concerns from my mind. I lifted the latch and burst outside to see the children waiting for me.

They all stood in an anxious bunch, the five girls and the boy still young enough to live at home: Evelyn, Sarah, Virgie, Mildred, and Grace in their nicest dresses, Evelyn holding baby Gary in her arms, and Sarah holding little Grace's hand. Doming stood behind them with an expression I could not read. But I did not care. I ran forward. Mildred was the first to cry, "Mama!" as she bounded for me. The rest followed in a cacophonous tangle of joyful shouts and little arms embracing me as we collided in the churchyard. Dizzy with happiness, I held each of them individually for a breathtaking hug before inspecting them one by one. Despite the relatively few days I'd been gone, I feared that they might have grown or changed in my absence.

The older girls stood back and examined me too, their happiness tinged with obvious worry. Mildred gently grasped my arms and exclaimed with horror, and Evelyn held my face in her hands, turning my chin this way and that to inspect what she found there.

"Mama Diamond," gasped Sarah with tears in her eyes, "what happened to you!"

I had forgotten what a mess I was. Long red scabs and purple bruises from my night of escape were still healing all over me. I didn't know until later that I was almost unrecognizable; my face was so swollen and discolored.

Evelyn shot a dark look at her father, and I realized that she believed Doming had done this to me. I could not let her think that. "It was the blade grass in the jungle, my dears, and nothing else. I walked through at night, so it cut me a bit. But I'm getting better now."

"You walked through the *jungle?"* exclaimed Evelyn. "You could have died! Mama, how did you—"

I quickly interrupted her. "Never mind that! You all look so pretty, and I'm so happy to see you!"

"What about these?" demanded Virgie, pointing to the many bruises. "Blade grass wouldn't make purple marks like this."

"I took a little tumble when I crossed the river," I said. This answer caused more consternation.

"You crossed the river?" my children asked questions all

at once. “Did you have to swim, Mama? Were there snakes in the water?”

“No, no,” I assured them. “As you can see...I am fine, and your baby brother or sister is well, too.”

They could see that I was not fine, but I was so happy to have them in my arms again that I did not care about bruises or cuts at all.

“Will you come home with us now, Mama?” asked Mildred.

“Mama come home!” Gary agreed, clinging to my legs.

I understood at that moment that I could not leave. I would never leave them. If they had not come here to find me, I suppose that the following day, I might have jumped out of the car on the way to Davao, the moment I fully understood what I was doing. Even if it meant having to live with Doming’s anger and abuse, I could not leave my children.

Doming, however, stood nearby with his head buried in his hands. It took us a little time to notice his silence, but at last, I stopped hugging and gazing at my children and turned my attention to him. I realized he was weeping. One by one, we all fell silent until Doming spoke.

“Forgive me,” he said gruffly, his voice rough with emotion. “If you can, please forgive me. Oh, Diamond, I’m so sorry for how I acted. Look at your poor face, my poor, beautiful Diamond! You did that all to escape me?”

“Yes,” I said hesitantly. I didn’t want to admit in front of our children that he’d threatened my life. Instead I said, “I never wanted to go. But after we argued, I felt I had no other choice."

The pastor stood nearby, protectively, ensuring that Doming kept his distance. But Doming didn't dare come close. He stayed back, wiping his face with his white handkerchief, shaking his head in dismay. "If you will please come home to us, I promise. I vow, before my family, and before this pastor who has cared for you these past days, never to harm you, Diamond. I won't raise my hand, or my voice, or ever make you afraid again."

Well, I had already realized I would never be able to leave. But hearing Doming gave me a sudden surge of hope. Could I believe him? Could things be alright again? With my children surrounding me, I thought hard.

"You vow before your children," I confirmed to Doming. "Including this little one who is not yet born?"

I rubbed the bump of our next child, who stirred inside me at the touch.

Doming's eyes lit with hope. "I vow it. I do."

"Then I will come home," I said to them all, and I was surrounded by cheers and shouting. Doming made no sound, but stood patiently still until I was ready to go stand beside him.

CHAPTER SEVENTEEN

# OUR LEGACY AND LIFE

Once Doming returned to his senses, he again became the man I had married. He was a man of his word. He kept his vow never to hurt or frighten me again. He never again accused me of infidelity. As kind and patient as he had been in the first days of our marriage, he was once more.

Soon after I returned home, our little Emmanuel was born, our second son. Doming doted on the baby. He felt that Emmanuel was a testament to the power of forgiveness. I was only too glad for the return of the life I had come to love, and the husband I had come to love as well.

With our family reunited, things quickly returned to normal for Doming's position of leadership. It was a simple matter for Doming to regain the respect of the town. Soon after, he was elected the mayor of Magpet, which included not just the town proper, but over twenty small villages in the surrounding area.

What a strange occurrence for me! As a tiny girl I had been the town's captured Japon oddity, roundly abused and mocked by the other children, despised or ignored by the adults. Now I was the mayor's wife, and my home was the largest house in town. Sometimes I had to shake my head in amazement.

For many years, Doming opened part of the Apostol house for use as a clinic, operated by visiting doctors from the nearest cities. There was always violence in the region around Magpet, vicious guerilla fighting for purposes that changed all the time. We saw severely wounded men brought in on hammocks, bleeding and groaning from machete fights and gunshot wounds. Those wounded in battle were not our only patients. Sometimes pregnant women or sick children came to us. Any medical emergency might bring someone into the clinic of the Apostol home.

I tried to hide the evidence of this violence from the children, but the arrival of such a patient, or many of them, was an unpredictable occurrence. Wounded men could be delivered at any hour of the day or night, with no warning, so Virgie, Mildred, and Grace certainly knew what was happening.

When things in the clinic became crowded, the great yawning basement housed some of these patients, and I knew that some people died down there. The doctors could not save everyone. This was yet another reason to find that chasm of the basement eerie and unapproachable.

I heard my little ones whisper about ghosts, and I assured

them that this could not be true. "We open our home to help others," I said. "No spirits are angry at us." But even I found the idea of stepping into the basement nerve-wracking. I had always believed it to be infested with snakes. Twice, observant little Mildred found snake skins in the yard, shed against a crack in the basement walls. One skin she found was almost ten feet long. We stared at it together in silent horror and then asked the gardeners to remove it.

"Will the snakes come into my room?" asked Mildred quietly.

"No, dear," I replied. "If there are snakes, they are happy to stay in the basement where there are plenty of bugs and mice to eat." I hoped this answer didn't worry her even more.

Doming once told me something disturbing. We were discussing the clinic, and how the number of wounded was increasing. Doming said, "In case of an emergency, you need to take the children into the basement shelter. You'll all be safer there."

"Oh, no!" I argued. "I can't take my babies down into that awful room – it's full of snakes and Heaven knows what else!"

"You certainly can't stay up here if guerilla troops invade Magpet and start shooting," he said, giving me a soothing hug. "Things are dangerous now, Diamond, and may grow worse in the coming years. Promise me you'll do the practical thing."

"Yes, I promise," I agreed half-heartedly. I prayed we would never have to do what he suggested.

In his job as mayor, Doming represented Magpet at regional and national meetings. I had no wish to attend those gatherings or try to mingle at parties or speak with political personalities. Erlinda accompanied her father instead, acting as the First Lady of Magpet. Sometimes I regretted that I could not rise to the occasion; more often, I was relieved that I would not have to try. Erlinda was far more suited to that life than I was. I knew where I belonged.

I thanked God for our second chance together, Doming's and mine. We had great times as a family. I have fond memories of so many happy incidents.

Every mango season, from April to June, Doming and several workers climbed the mango trees in the backyard to pick the matured mangoes. The bounty was amazing; there were almost thirty mango trees on the property. Sometimes the workers shook the trees so the ripened mangoes fell. The children rushed in to grab these sweet fruits and gobble them up. Then the men hand-washed the raw mangoes and lined them up in the storage room. After a few weeks, the mangoes deepened into ripeness, a rich golden yellow. The maids served the ripe mangoes at the breakfast table each morning, adding their sunshine to our lives even on rainy days. Mildred, in particular, loved the fruit and looked forward to the season.

One summer the Philippines were hit with a particularly violent typhoon. The whole family and all the servants huddled together downstairs in the large social hall, listening to the wind and rain lash the walls outside. All the windows were boarded and protected, but the storm made such a fierce sound that the little ones were afraid. "Nothing to fear!" Doming told them. "We are having a campout inside, that's all!" Then he gathered them into big hugs and told stories the whole time, making everyone laugh.

Doming owned the biggest stereo in town. He was a fan of Frank Sinatra and Nat King Cole, so he had an impressive collection of their albums. Their songs could be heard all over the house as he enjoyed them; the children knew all the words even though these men sang in English. Doming regularly had guests over at the house on late afternoons, to enjoy some drinks while listening to the music.

I remember when the installers came with those massive stereo components. The stereo system was surely the most modern and powerful entertainment device that had ever come to Magpet—and when they turned it on, it overpowered the generator and shut down the town's source of electricity for hours. Mildred, a schoolgirl at the time, was so embarrassed; her friends all wanted to know why her father had shut off Magpet's electricity.

Doming was respected and admired by all, not just as a leader of the Bagobo tribe, but also for his devotion to his family. He often let Mildred sit on his lap while he held council meetings with the elders, never shooing any of his children away or ignoring their presence.

Doming made sure that all his children went to church. Each Sunday, he rose early and played with the young children on our big bed, tickling and wrestling with them. After breakfast, he ordered everyone to take a shower and prepare for church.

Now it was time for the ritual they all knew by heart. Doming lined them up, oldest to youngest, to be certain everyone was properly dressed. "Tuck in that shirt, Gary!" he teased, adjusting Gary's stray shirttail. "This ribbon looks a little cockeyed," he might tell Mildred or Virgie, straightening their lop-sided bows. One by one, he went down the line, using his own pomade as hair gel and carefully combing everyone's hair. He was precise about parting each child's hair straight down the middle. I had to hide my smile as he fussed over them. The children hated the pomade, I knew, but they so loved their father's attention that they stood straight and proud under his ministrations, until he said, "Very good! You are ready for church!"

When it came to his children, Doming had endless patience and kindness. No matter how busy or tired he might have been, he never complained about rising in the middle of the night to fetch a glass of water if one of the kids called for it, or to reassure anyone who had bad dreams. Whenever one of them felt sick, he carried the child on his shoulder to the doctor's office. To raise their spirits afterward, he always stopped by the candy store on the way back home.

At night, Doming stayed up late helping the children with their schoolwork and assignments. Math was always his favorite subject, so math tutoring was particularly enjoyable for him as well as educational for them. During end-of-year award ceremonies, he attended every event, present when each of his children received an honor ribbon. Afterward, with the ribbon pinned on the lucky child's shirt, we all celebrated their successes together. Doming treated everyone to a nice meal out to commemorate all that hard work. Doming truly cherished being able to spend time with the children that way. Watching their achievements filled him with pride.

Some of my fondest memories are when Doming and I watched our children whiling away long afternoons in the shade of the great duhat tree on the back lawn. They tumbled around, playing games and singing. It looked like the perfect picture of happiness to me, yet the strangeness of this scene filled me with wonder. I remembered so many years before, when I was hardly older than Virgie was now, when I sat under that same tree keeping careful watch over Rodolfo, Orlando, and Rachel until their nanny called for them to come inside for bath time and I was sent off to do other chores. Under the shade of that tree, as the lowest servant in the house, I had first learned to love this family.

Our older children were adults now.

Erlinda, of course, had long been married and living with her own family. I never considered her my daughter in the same way I thought of Rachel, Evelyn, or Sarah, and I doubt she wanted that kind of relationship with me. But she was still part of my life.

Erlinda and her husband's relationship was far from perfect. They lived in a separate home a few yards away from the Apostol home, and frequently we heard them screaming back and forth at each other. Though the matters that caused them to argue were often trivial, they fought viciously, hurling insults and enraged accusations. We often heard their children in the background of these terrible arguments, wailing in fear.

Doming normally avoided interfering in the couple's squabbles, but one day, he could no longer tolerate it. He said,

"I'm going to take care of this once and for all!" I followed him in concern as he stormed through the house, snatching up a container of kerosene as he went.

When I realized what he was about to do, I begged Doming to let go of the container. I knew full well what could happen when Doming's temper got away from him. But he didn't hear a word I said. He was so furious about their behavior, so livid about the cries of Doming's beloved grandchildren, that I could not stop him, though I tried my hardest.

When he burst into Erlinda and Rudy's house, right before their eyes, Doming flung the kerosene all over the floor. He snapped out a match and was about to light it, when he came to his senses, breathing hard, but under control once more. Erlinda and Rudy stared at him in astonished fright.

"This fighting stops," Doming commanded, "or I will burn your house to the ground!"

His ferocity must have convinced them that he meant what he said. No longer did we hear fighting coming from Erlinda and Rudy's house. I suppose they might have continued to fight, but if so, it was done quietly.

Dodong had always wanted to sail the world. After he went to college, he served on a cargo ship for a few years before he married his girlfriend. Dodong's marriage was a grandiose affair, which Doming paid for himself, supplying food and drinks to a party that lasted a week.

Rodolfo and Orlando also went away to school in Davao, but neither of them was as strong as Dodong. Regretfully I realized that their mother's abandonment had profoundly affected them. They carried their insecurities with them.

Rodolfo had little interest in school. He returned to Magpet as soon as he could, to spend his time goofing around town with his friends.

Orlando studied finance, though he remained uncertain about what he wanted to do after graduation. He and his father had several talks about what he should do with his life. Orlando, like Doming, was handsome and popular, so he dated many women in Davao and in Magpet. He often asked his young sisters to deliver gifts to his Magpet girlfriends.

Rachel, too, carried the scars of feeling unwanted. This broke my heart because Rachel had grown up as beautiful and intelligent as her parents. She was the kindest, most loving young woman, always gently mediating between her siblings when there were arguments. But she never overcame the feeling of being a child abandoned on the front steps of her house, waiting for Adela to return. My bright Rachel went to Cebu for college where she finished with a degree in pharmacy.

My Evelyn remained strong-willed and fearless. When she was sixteen, her school chose her as homecoming queen. In preparation for the pageant, artistic Dodong was commissioned to paint the stage background, which was quite an undertaking. Doming supported the project by buying all the painting materials. Doming shone with pride for both Dodong and Evelyn, telling everyone in town about their accomplishments.

Since the homecoming queen was featured in a parade through the town, Doming had a very elegant float built for Evelyn. Unfortunately, her escort had a severe toothache at the time of the parade, which delayed the show for a few hours, but Doming quickly brought the boy home and tended to his pain, helping him recover enough to continue the festivities. I can only imagine him thinking, *no boy with a toothache is going to ruin my daughter's big day!* Doming also hosted a grand party afterward.

Evelyn was beautiful like Adela and intelligent like Doming. Emotionally, she was close to her sister Rachel, and as soon as she was old enough, she joined Rachel in Cebu, where they went to college together. Evelyn studied to become a nurse. When I saw my daughters reaching out for their education, it made me terribly proud. I wanted them to have all the opportunities and success they could find.

Doming believed strongly in the power of education and never hesitated to tell others about the achievements of his brilliant daughters. He often spoke with anticipation about how the younger children would someday amaze us as well. Anyone in town who met up with Doming knew that before any business was conducted, they must listen to an update on the Apostol children.

Evelyn and Rachel loved coming home from college during the holidays. The younger children looked forward with delight to their visits because their big sisters always brought presents for the younger siblings. Their visits were like a grand slumber party; all the sisters spread sleeping bags around the living room and stayed up late into the night, playing games and singing.

Rachel had a special gift for communicating with and inspiring young people. I wondered if her difficult childhood had taught her empathy and kindness that others responded well to. She started youth groups in Magpet that encouraged community service. Around Magpet, Rachel and Evelyn were both popular, so they hosted fundraising events and parties. A long string of single men sought their attention, as you might expect, but their hopes of snagging a beautiful, intelligent Apostol daughter amounted to nothing. Neither girl had time for serious romance; they were focused on their educations.

Sarah, the youngest of Doming and Adela's children, grew up quiet. She held her feelings inside her. She was like me, in that way. She and I were close both in friendship and mutual understanding, and we could share entire exchanges with just one look or a patient smile.

I became aware that Sarah was slipping out of the house on weekends, often with small bags of groceries or gifts. I guessed she took things to share with her friends, or maybe even that she had a boyfriend. Then I noticed that she sometimes allowed Virgie or Mildred to accompany her. I doubted she would let her much-younger sisters join her on social calls, so my curiosity grew.

I asked Virgie and Mildred where they went with Sarah. Both girls knew not to lie to me—I was a keen observer and knew very well when my children tried to slip a fib past me. They stayed loyal to Sarah in this case, however. "Mama, Sarah takes us to visit a friend. They just talk, and we play with the little boy who lives there. But she asked us not to say the friend's name."

It seemed strange to me that this was something kept so

secret. What was the harm in visiting a friend? So finally I asked Sarah directly.

Sarah looked like she wanted to be honest with me. "But you have to promise not to tell Papa," she said.

I was afraid of making a promise like that, but Sarah was my daughter, and I had to protect her. So I said, "Now that depends. You're not in any trouble or danger, are you?"

Sarah shook her head vehemently. "No, I'm in no danger, but she might be if Papa learns the truth."

"She?"

"My mother. Adela. She has moved back to the area. She doesn't want Papa to know, and she keeps mostly to herself. But there is a child, a son she had by her lover. A little half-brother to me. I want to visit her, Mama Diamond. I love her."

"Of course you love her," I said with complete understanding. I knew very well that it was possible for someone to make terrible mistakes but still be forgiven, for Doming and I had been through a similar ordeal.

None of Adela's other children had ever forgiven her for abandoning them when they were young and their father was in prison. It had been Adela's decision to go, so I could understand their anger, but how terrible, for six of her seven children to refuse to speak to her. How could I deny her a relationship with her youngest daughter? I told Sarah, "I will say nothing to Doming. There is no need. And you may send Adela my best wishes, too. But Sarah..."

"Yes, Mama Diamond?"

"Doming has workers everywhere, dozens of men who report to him. I doubt that Adela can keep her presence a secret forever. You might tell her that. Maybe...I don't know, maybe telling him the truth would be best."

"No, no. Mama Adela insists it must be secret. She worries for the safety of her son."

I could not imagine Doming ever harming a child—but then again, not long ago, he had threatened to kill me while I was pregnant. That time was over, and I had forgiven him. He was a changed man. Still, I could easily understand how Adela might be afraid. So I agreed to be silent on the entire matter. In the end, I did not think it was my decision to make.

Sarah continued to visit her mother, with my implicit blessing. In my heart, I always believed families should be connected.

After Emmanuel's happy birth, Doming and I had one more child, our baby Josephine, in 1970. Those were blissful years for me, surrounded by my large family—and what an amazing span of ages they were: from Dodong, a grown man traveling the world and having a grand marriage, to little Josephine, just an infant in my arms.

The same year Josephine was born, Doming traveled back to his birth town of Cebu to take care of his family's estate. While there, he happened to run into his third cousin, Inday. He was astonished to see her and asked immediately how she was—if she was content—and what had become of their child Simplicio. Inday reassured him, and told him everything.

After Doming was forced out of Cebu, Inday married a local man who adopted Simplicio as his own. Simplicio was the only child they ever had together. Simplicio grew up well provided for, and loved by his mother and stepfather. This all came as a tremendous relief to Doming.

"You must meet Simplicio!" Inday said. "You should know each other." Thus, Doming got his wish to reunite with the son he was forced to leave behind.

Simplicio was a successful lawyer practicing in Cebu (as Doming had once been), and was married with three children of his own. He was the spitting image of Doming: no one could mistake that this was his son. Doming was overjoyed to find out that Simplicio was thriving, and especially that this long-lost son had never harbored any ill feelings toward him.

When Doming came home, he happily shared the news with us. The children exclaimed, "We have new cousins in Cebu! What are they like? Can they come over to play? Can we go and visit them?"

I thought Doming looked years younger, as if a weight had been lifted from his shoulders. I knew that the question of Simplicio had always worried him, but especially as Doming grew older, his concern had grown deeper. Seeing our Dodong as an adult, living his dreams, had especially reminded Doming that he had another son in the world whom he never had the honor of knowing. Now, the assurance that Simplicio was well, successful, and forgiving was the perfect antidote to Doming's anxiety.

CHAPTER EIGHTEEN

# THE DANGEROUS ROAD

In 1974, my faith was tested once more.

The political situation in the Philippines was tumultuous. But again, we were far from the capital city. Though Doming was the mayor, I remained uninvolved in politics. I lived in a home I seldom had to leave, and even when I did, bodyguards accompanied and protected me. I didn't understand all of it until the trouble landed on my doorstep.

Doming took some of his guards and went away for a business trip. This wasn't unusual, since he had become mayor. The day he was meant to return, we planned our usual celebratory welcome for him. The children were excited to see their Papa again, and I, too, was happy that Doming was coming home.

Yet as we prepared, we all heard a strange alarm rising up from the streets of Magpet. I went to the front door and looked outside, to see people racing around, shouting. Clearly, something terrible had happened. I felt my stomach drop with worry. The situation felt eerily similar to that day when we'd learned that Doming was going to prison for murdering tenants...yet the expressions of the Magpet people were more frightened this time. It was as if now, they also feared for their own lives.

"Mama, what's happening?" asked Virgie.

"I don't know," I said quietly. I looked around, trying to find someone who could help. "Virgie, my dear, stay inside while I go ask. Close the door behind me and lock it, and I'll be right back."

Steeling my nerves, I stepped out into the yard. None of the servants were around; they'd all run into the roads outside the estate to join the fracas. I couldn't imagine what caused the fear in their eyes. Heedlessly, I rushed up to the intersection. I saw a Bagobo tribesman I recognized. "Please!" I called. "Tell me what is happening!"

"Diamon," he said, his face turning ashen with dismay. "It's not my place."

Many people rushed down the road that led out of town. I feared they were fleeing from something. Another memory flashed back to me—worse, even, than the day when Doming had gone to prison. A memory of people packing, preparing to run away...a voice sending me outside to play so I wouldn't be underfoot...then crashes, cries of fear, and shouting, which I heard from my hiding place beneath a bamboo floor.

I felt faint for a moment, then snapped myself out of it. I couldn't be weak now. My children were in the house. I commanded the Bagobo man. "Tell me what is happening, right now, please!"

"About ten miles outside of town," he said, gesturing toward the road. "There has been an ambush by guerrillas. They shot everyone in the car...Diamon, it was...it was Doming, and his bodyguards."

I shook my head in confusion. "They were shot? Doming was shot? Where is he? Can I see him? Have they been taken to a hospital?"

The man's face told me more than his words had. But I still let myself believe for just a moment longer. Mere days before, I had kissed Doming goodbye, and watched as he hugged each of the children and promised souvenirs from his travels.

"Can they be saved?" I asked once more, my hope slipping even as the words escaped me.

The man lowered his head in grief. "Diamon, they are all dead."

My life has always been one of sudden, sweeping changes. Time and again, upheaval has left me reeling as I sought purchase on new ground. Now once more, an act of terrible violence had changed everything. Doming was dead, at the hands of guerillas—very much like the way my parents had died.

Everyone in the family came home from far and wide across the Philippines for Doming's funeral. In the Philippines, body viewings ordinarily last for several days. Doming's went on for about two weeks, for a number of reasons. We wanted to make certain that all his relatives, especially his children, could come to pay their respects. Friends and business associates came from great distances for the viewing. The governor of Cotabato arrived with his armed guards. There were so many flowers that the smell of warm petals lingered for days after the internment. Doming's body, having been riddled with bullets, began to bloat – but somehow, his face retained its handsome features.

Doming's first son, Simplicio, had never visited Magpet before. He made the long, stressful, sometimes dangerous journey from Cebu to attend his father's funeral. Despite our sadness, we welcomed him warmly into our home. Seeing him was a shock, because while all of Doming's sons resembled their father to some extent, Simplicio was simply Doming made over. His resemblance to Doming broke my heart, but also gave me a measure of comfort, reminding me that Doming would live on through his children.

Simplicio was amazed to meet his half-siblings. Of course, Erlinda and Dodong were fairly close to his age, but Orlando, Rodolfo, Rachel, Evelyn, and Sarah were young adults, and my children even younger, little Josephine still in diapers. "I knew I had little brothers and sisters," Simplicio joked with them, "but I didn't consider how very little they might be!"

At once, he grew deeply fond of Mildred, who was the same age as Simplicio's only daughter. Perhaps he hoped to ease my burden a bit; he offered to take Mildred back to Cebu with him. "She'll be my adopted daughter," he explained.

"I'll care for her like my own little girl."

But I could not bear the thought of it—especially not after losing Doming. While Mildred loved her oldest half-brother at once, she, too, was frightened by the idea of leaving Magpet for a new home.

"It is a kind offer," I assured Simplicio, "and I know you would look after Mildred, but I cannot be separated from my babies."

Poor Evelyn, who had always been her "Papa's girl," was devastated by her father's death. She didn't want to return to college and might have stayed in Magpet permanently, except for Erlinda's insistence that she get back to her education.

I had no time to grieve for my husband. Even during his funeral, I kept my tears to myself. All I could wonder was how I was to provide for my children. The last time Doming had disappeared from our lives, things had fallen apart, and I feared the same would happen again. Was I selfish to deny Mildred a more stable home in Cebu? I wondered about that after Simplicio left us...but the only thing worse than my grief and worry was the idea of losing one of my children, even if to a loving home.

You might wonder how it could happen, that I was abruptly in such dire need. Was I not the wife of the mayor, the lady of House Apostol? Even I was uncertain how to answer this. My circumstances were always so strange and unpredictable that any shift in the earth might set it all spinning. Everything I had, everything I was, was tied inexorably to being Doming's wife. Without Doming, what was I?

Too much was lost, too much was at stake. Perhaps I was entitled to certain things but did not have the education or experience to manage them. Without Doming's protection, I became once more what I had always been: a foreign oddity, a person with no real place in the world, who was nevertheless responsible for others who relied upon me.

Meanwhile, our six young children lost their papa to sudden terrible violence, and I had few answers for them. Only Virgie and Mildred were old enough to really grasp what their father's death meant. The younger ones did not even understand that Papa would never return. Grace had terrible nightmares that guerrillas were coming to kill her, and that her Papa was their tormented prisoner who needed to be rescued. "Your Papa is at peace now," I reassured her when she came to me in tears. "He has gone to Heaven to be with Jesus."

Again and again Gary asked me, "When is Papa coming home?" even though I gently and repeatedly explained, fighting my own tears, that Papa could not come home again. To Gary, death had no permanence yet. Emmanuel and Josephine, still just babies, only knew that their Mama and siblings were heartbroken, and that their loving Papa no longer held them in his arms.

One day I sought some time alone to sort through my confused thoughts. I wandered the yard, dry-eyed, though my body felt sore and breathless as if I wept anyway. I meandered around the grounds, unaware of my surroundings, and eventually wandered toward the front entryway.

"Diamond," said a strangely familiar voice, like something from a daydream. It took me a moment to look up. When I did, I had a bit of a start, for there stood Adela. She was many years older than when I last saw her, but her face remained lovely despite a few weary lines around her eyes. She stood outside the grounds, composed, in a simple day dress, her hands folded in front of her. Though her clothing was inexpensive, she still carried an aura of elegance.

"I suppose I should call you Mrs. Apostol," she said. Her tone was solemn but kind; she wasn't mocking me. Considering her own words, she said, "How strange. Life is very strange, don't you think?"

I honestly did not know what to do for a moment. Even though I worked for her throughout my childhood, our interactions were extremely limited. To me, she was unapproachable. Now here I stood as the lady of the house, in title alone, and feeling as lost as the day I had first met Adela, when I was a little girl.

She began to explain herself. "I wanted to visit. Doming's death is such a shock. I was afraid of him, you know. Afraid for my son. Sarah probably told you. I suppose I don't need to be afraid now. But I don't wish to offend you. Your loss is terrible. I am sorry for you, and so...am I making any sense?"

I nodded mutely.

Her eyes wandered over the Apostol house with nostalgia. "The place hasn't changed much on the outside. I used to watch the street from that window there. I used to scold the groundskeeper about the state of the front lawn."

Then she turned her attention fully back to me. "When I heard Doming had married you, I was so surprised...but not angry, not at all. I remembered how well you cared for the children. You were their mother when I was not. That's what mattered to me. I thought, *better he marries that kind girl Diamond than a stranger who does not care about my children.*"

She gave a brittle laugh. "You must wonder about that. You ask yourself how I could care about my children when I ran away from them. I can hardly explain it myself...well, perhaps I shouldn't have come. I'll leave you alone."

"No, wait," I said, suddenly finding my voice. "You only surprised me. Please, it's nice to talk to someone. I have only the children now, and not many friends."

"You know that Sarah visits me often?" It was not a question. "I know your girls Virgie and Mildred quite well, even little Grace. They are lovely children. How are they handling things?"

I bowed my head. "It is very difficult for them. They adored their Papa, and they are devastated, but also worried for me. Virgie tries so hard to be mature and handle the little ones to help me out...but she's just a child herself."

"Virgie is a sharp one. I see Doming in your daughters, but they're like you too: even-tempered, thoughtful, and alert. I always noticed that about you. You never missed anything. My other maids dithered about, gossiping and forgetting things. Not Diamond."

I had never dreamed of speaking to Adela at all, much

less speaking to her with frankness. But life had become so strange—as Adela herself had said—and so alien to me in the past weeks, that nothing seemed impossible. I stepped closer and confided, "I didn't know you paid any attention to me at all."

Adela shrugged. "That's fair enough. My mind was seldom on anything but the business of being lady of the house. But the children always talked about you. I just...ah, it was such a long time ago, when I had a powerful father doting on me, when everything was leisurely, when Doming and I were truly in love..." Her face changed; she looked a bit horrified. "That was unkind of me. I'm sorry."

"No, no," I insisted. "I like to hear about it."

"Not jealous at all?" she asked. "What an unusual woman you are. I admire that. Tell me, did you love Doming? He was twice your age, maybe more, and I know how difficult he could be. Don't worry about speaking ill of the dead. It's just you and me talking. I'll understand."

Her forwardness was fascinating. No one else ever dared to say such things to me. Yet I felt safe talking to her. Her face spoke of experiences, regrets, and hard-won empathy, qualities that are only gained through suffering. So I answered her question. "Yes, I did love him—most of the time—and yes, he was difficult. But he was also special in many ways. I wonder if special people are always difficult. I don't know. Now I grieve as much for the loss of my children's father as I do for my husband."

Adela listened to me thoughtfully. "Then you and I have some things in common. Both of us lost and alone. Shall I visit you again, Diamond?"

"I would like that. Yes, please." Suddenly, the idea of a friendship with Adela seemed perfectly natural. My world had grown so odd.

After saying goodbye to Adela, even clasping her hand in a token of friendship, I wandered back toward the house. As I did, I looked up to the windows of the house next door and saw Erlinda watching, her face set in stony anger. Erlinda was her father's daughter through and through, and had long ago washed her hands of anything to do with Adela. She clearly did not want her birth mother anywhere near the Apostol home. I was so weary, though, that I could not bring myself to care.

Doming's death brought dramatic changes to us, and to the town of Magpet as well. A new town mayor was appointed. Once more, without Doming at the head of the tribes, the household was threatened with chaos.

One might wonder how Doming could have left us this way, especially knowing the dangers of the region in which we lived. He did have a small life insurance policy, but that money did not last long. He had assumed, if disaster happened, we would always be looked after by the older children, especially Erlinda, and that his properties generated enough income to keep us comfortable.

Unfortunately, he did not realize how things would deteriorate in his absence. Doming had arranged for all his properties to be mine upon his death, so I owned a significant amount of farmland. Unfortunately, I had no head for business, and Doming had never taught me anything about rents, finances, or the obligations of the estate. These things were always in Erlinda's hands. And so, indeed, Erlinda took over management of the estate and all of its incoming money. In the family hierarchy—which was the most important thing—she was in charge because Doming had trained her to be.

My role reverted to servant once more, though I had never really stopped being a part of the household duties, many of which I enjoyed. As weeks went by, I took over more household chores in Erlinda's home in exchange for compensation. When that was not enough, I asked Erlinda if I could farm a piece of land so I could sell the crops. Erlinda consented to this. I had no money to pay laborers, so I manually tilled the land myself. I had done so before.

I know how this sounds, as if Erlinda was purposely withholding money from us. Erlinda's feelings for me had never been affectionate, but I know she cared for my children because they were her half-siblings. In fairness, Erlinda was under tremendous financial strain. During those years she paid for college for Rodolfo, Rachel, and Evelyn.

Without Doming heading things, some of the tenants "forgot" to pay their rent, and much of our expected profits disappeared into someone else's pockets. Money simply wasn't coming in like it did when Doming was in charge. Erlinda had a great head for business, but she also had a large family under her care without much assistance, and she was not feared as Doming had been.

Events unfolded with eerie similarity to the time when Doming had gone away to prison. The servants and luxuries disappeared as soon as the money did. The children and I moved into a smaller set of rooms in the great house, a size that we could maintain.

I did get financial help from my older stepchildren. Dodong's own family was growing, but he helped me whenever he could. By then Evelyn, bless her heart, was earning a living as a nurse. She slipped money to me on the side, never letting Erlinda know. "What she doesn't know won't hurt her," Evelyn would say with a wink. She was never afraid of Erlinda. In fact, Evelyn may have been the only person besides Doming himself who could hush Erlinda's tirades. And dear Evelyn always stood up for me.

After college, Rachel joined the Campus Crusade for Christ organization. Her work there sent her to various cities away from Magpet, so she did not see us often. Orlando began a job in Davao, and rarely visited Magpet.

Sarah in particular seemed to be a target for Erlinda's bullying. Erlinda constantly scolded her youngest sister. And between wanting to be loyal to the Apostol legacy, to her mother Adela, and to me and her half-siblings, Sarah was already emotionally conflicted. She tried so hard to weather the storm, but she was still hardly more than a child herself. The stress of Erlinda's ire simply wore her down. There had always been an ugly rumor that Sarah was not Doming's daughter, but the child of Adela's lover, and I sometimes wondered if Erlinda believed that. Doming never believed it himself, or at least, he did not care. He loved Sarah as his own.

Erlinda rode Sarah ruthlessly. Sarah wanted to leave home so badly. She married her high school boyfriend when she was only eighteen. I firmly believe she rushed the relationship just to escape from home and Erlinda's rule.

Erlinda and I had never been friends. For many years I sensed that she disapproved of her father's marriage to me. She believed he could have had a much finer wife, someone who was his social equal, or otherwise that he'd had no need to marry again after Adela left.

Though she loved her young half-siblings in her own brusque way, she was so much like her father in temperament. My children were intelligent and well-behaved, and seldom needed to be corrected for anything beyond simple, childish mistakes. Doming never struck them because his children were his greatest joy, and I would never raise a hand to them, because I had suffered that myself as a child.

Erlinda had no such qualms. Her temper could flare, and she could become abusive. She didn't hesitate to smack my children's hands or yank at their ears if something annoyed her, no matter how many people were watching. Though the culture was fairly accepting of physical punishment for children (at the time, though that is no longer the case today), her reasons seemed outlandish to me. Erlinda lashed out for ridiculous things. When she resorted to slapping their faces, it was too much.

After I saw Virgie's cheek flaming, I went directly to Erlinda to intervene. "Don't strike your brothers and sisters," I said. "If they do something wrong, tell me. I'm their mother and I'll take care of the discipline."

"You don't discipline them at all," she countered. "It was

preposterous how Papa spoiled them all. Now they must face the realities of life."

That was a fine statement, from someone as spoiled as Erlinda had been. I almost felt like laughing. Instead I said, "Spoiled or not, I will discipline them—not you."

This curbed the worst of her behavior, but one could never be completely certain what Erlinda might do next.

I tried to understand. I asked God to help me understand. Erlinda's life had not been an easy one. As privileged as she was, she had endured stresses and grief that had hardened her. Often I wondered what hurt she held inside to make her behave this way toward us. I know that she grieved for her father. They had been so close. Perhaps that, combined with the stress of supporting two families, was simply too much for her.

As I slept fitfully one night, dreaming an old, fuzzy dream of red rain and screams, I realized that Virgie was shaking me awake. "Mama! Mama! There's gunfire nearby!" I heard it at once. It sounded as if a military encounter with the guerillas had spilled into the town of Magpet, as Doming had once warned me could happen. I darted out of bed. "Keep low," I said to Virgie, taking her hand. "We must wake your brothers and sisters and get to the basement."

Virgie did not argue. We met Mildred in the hall; she, too, had been on her way to find me. "Quickly, girls. Help me get everyone up."

With every second, the gunfire sounded closer. Grace was

terrified; she'd only gotten over her nightmares a few weeks before. As we moved fast, crouched below the windows, my three oldest girls helped me with Gary, Emmanuel, and Josephine, who began to cry in fear—first at being woken so abruptly, then at the sounds of gunfire. "Shh, hush now," I whispered. "We're going to do what your Papa said, and it will keep us safe."

The seven of us hurried in breathless silence down to the kitchen, and from there we entered the basement. Mildred balked for only a moment, saying, "Mama, the snakes!" But she understood that snakes were little to fear compared to flying bullets. She put on a brave face and took Josephine's hand to help her with the steps.

There was no light down there save for a couple of candles and some matches that were practically too damp to light. Near the rough staircase was old furniture—I didn't let myself think of what vermin might be living inside. In the flickering candlelight, the children and I huddled, shivering, as the gunfire continued outside. Whenever the children grew too frightened, I said, "Don't worry. Your Papa is watching over us. We will be all right." I did not want them to know that I was just as terrified as they were. Huddling there underneath a terrible fight brought back the sickening, confusing memories from the most awful moment of my childhood. I clutched my children and prayed silently.

And indeed, we survived the night, and emerged back into daylight together, the fighting over for the moment.

CHAPTER NINETEEN

# THROUGH THE DARKNESS

Erlinda and her husband Rudy behaved themselves out of fear of Doming's wrath while he was alive. Once he died, their tendency to fight returned in full force. Their constant bickering not only happened in their house, but it also occurred inside the Apostol home, in front of my children. Nothing pleased Erlinda at that point. Her temper flared out of control on several occasions.

One day Rudy decided to prove his worth as a chef by making peanut brittle, with peanuts freshly harvested from his family's farm. He spent hours in our kitchen preparing the treat while all of the young children eagerly awaited its completion. Finally, after much anticipation, Rudy declared that the peanut brittle was ready, and began laying the pieces out on banana leaves so they could cool.

Unfortunately, though, in his excitement he made the

mistake of joking about Erlinda's lack of culinary skills, which did not sit well with her at all. She erupted in a fury, and without hesitation chucked handfuls of peanut brittle out of the window in rage. Everyone stood speechless while watching their beloved treats thrown away in an instant, thanks to one careless joke gone wrong.

I did what I could to make money, taking in laundry, and cooking for workers when they came to town for a building project. I raised two farm hogs to sell so I could pay for the children's school supplies. I sold one of them and set the money aside for just that purpose. Not long after that, while I was washing clothes in the river, my daughter Mildred came running out of the woods.

"Mama," she said breathlessly. "Erlinda wants to borrow the money you got from selling our hog. I'm supposed to ask you where you've hidden it, so I can bring it to her."

I shook my head in distress. Why did Erlinda need my money? I couldn't imagine what use she'd have for that small amount. But Mildred looked truly upset.

"Is Erlinda angry?" I asked. Mildred nodded, biting her lip. "All right, then." I described the drawer where I'd stashed my meager treasure. Mildred raced away. Clearly Erlinda had worried her.

When later I came home with my baskets of laundry to hang for drying, Mildred waited, looking no less worried, and as if she'd been crying. "What happened, dear?"

"Erlinda said I took too long," Mildred sniffled. "She took the money from me and threw it across the room. She screamed so loud it scared me, and Virgie came running to see if someone was hurt. Why did Erlinda do that, Mama?"

"She has a temper, like your Papa," I replied, because I had no other answer.

"But Papa never smacked me," said Mildred.

Episodes like that made me ache for the power to escape our situation. But each time I thought about escaping, I was met with the same problem: escape to where? To do what? Saving money was so hard; anyone with children knows as soon as one thing is paid for, another thing is needed.

I do not wish to make it sound like Erlinda was the villain of my life. Circumstances were more responsible for my plight than she was. Sometimes Erlinda could be a different person. She enjoyed going to the movies in a nearby town with a cinema, and always took Mildred along with her. As clever as she was, Erlinda could be quite funny and witty. In many ways, I was still in awe of her. Life was not easy in Magpet, and perhaps she did the best she could.

Erlinda was family. The culture we lived in stressed the importance of family above everything else. I only wished Erlinda would remember that when her temper got the better of her.

Erlinda's husband, Rudy, was a man of many faces. On most occasions, he came across as a kindhearted man and loving parent, but he had a dark side that endangered my daughters. I began to sense it as Virgie and Mildred grew up. He loved to chase my girls around. When he managed to catch one of them, he smothered them with his whiskers. Though it appeared to be innocent game-playing, there was something about his actions that set off alarm bells in my head.

My suspicions were confirmed one day when Virgie and Mildred came to me with frightened faces and told me what had happened. They said that Rudy had lured them into playing a "secret adult game" on separate occasions—something they knew shouldn't happen between children and adults.

My heart sank at their words. What kind of man would take advantage of such innocence? Immediately I sat down with both girls and made sure they promised to never again go near Rudy without an adult present. They must also keep an eye out for each other whenever playing outside or walking around our small town alone. After making sure my girls understood how serious the situation really was, I went in search of Rudy.

I doubt he ever expected me to speak to him like I did. I was normally quiet around him, but when it came to my daughters, I could not sit idly by. Rudy thought we were vulnerable without Doming to protect us. He saw my daughters as easy prey and apparently didn't believe I would do anything. Like some people before, he mistook my quiet for weakness.

I caught him alone outside and spoke where no one else

could hear us. I noticed immediately that he had trouble meeting my eyes. He realized at once that I was seriously upset. I knew exactly what I risked in confronting him, yet I'd rather be homeless than have my girls living in a place where they faced such vile treatment.

"We are a family," I told him, "and I respect that you are Erlinda's husband. But what you are doing to my girls is wrong. You will not do it again. I won't stand for it."

He said almost exactly what I had expected. "I don't know what you're talking about. I like playing with the kids. So what? Did I scare one of them?"

I refused to let him deflect me. "I won't mince words with you, Rudy. I do not wish to disrupt our family more than it already has been. But unless you want your wife and her brothers to know what you have been up to, you'll keep well away from my daughters."

"Don't threaten me in my own home," he retorted hotly. "This is some nonsense your daughters have concocted to get even with me, just because I scolded them for— "

"This is my only warning!" I interrupted, more loudly than I'd expected to. I was not accustomed to confrontations. My own ferocity was strong enough to startle me. I trembled with it. I hadn't known it was possible to be that full of rage. For a moment I understood how Doming managed to kill three men in anger. Maybe Rudy saw this is my face, because he pulled back, regarding me with dumbfounded shock.

Keeping my voice steady, I added my only remaining threat. "If I hear one more thing about this behavior, I will tell your wife, and then Dodong. I'll tell Orlando and Rodolfo.

I will tell Simplicio in Cebu. They all love their little sisters, and Erlinda is not the only one who inherited their father's temper."

I left him standing there. I had to return to the house and sit in the dark for a while, to calm myself before I faced my children again. Hours seemed to pass before I could collect myself.

One day, Gary complained of a painful stomachache. He groaned as he lay on his side, twisting on his bed with sweat beading his forehead. I immediately panicked. I had no money or resources to get him medical help. All I could do was give him whatever relief I could provide at home. Yet his condition only worsened. With no other choice, I took him to the clinic, knowing we had nothing with which to pay for his treatment.

Upon our arriving there, a kind doctor saw our plight and decided to take care of Gary without asking for payment in return. After some tests, he informed me that if I had delayed bringing Gary for care by just another day, there could have been serious consequences.

I thanked God for the generosity of the doctor, and for giving me the foresight to take Gary for treatment in time to avoid disaster. I saw this event as a sign that God still protected us in our greatest need. My stepchildren were also able to help us, and I thanked God that they had grown up to be such kind and generous people.

Years passed in this deteriorating situation. Some periods of time were better than others. My children often had academic successes to celebrate. Having my family together under one roof was a blessing I never discounted. No matter how tired I felt, I remembered that at least we had somewhere to call home.

Indeed, there was something truly special about coming home, knowing I'd done my best. I loved joining my children to learn what their day had been like, what had happened at school or with their friends. Many years ago, I had made dinnertime important to my adopted family, gathering Dodong, Rodolfo, Orlando, and Rachel over a meager meal to "play house," and that ritual had held us together. So it was now. Brother Tim had put an idea into my head many years before, to gather such golden moments wherever they might be. Being a family at the dinner table was one of life's great pleasures.

The biggest problem was that we could never get ahead of our poverty. There was never enough money, yet there were always more expenses. Finally, we decided to rent the Apostol house out to tenants. There were enough rooms to have several renters at once, and the generated income would be a big help. However, this came with a daunting prospect: we would have to move into Erlinda and Rudy's home, to live with them and their children. How could I agree to such a thing, after Rudy had proven himself so untrustworthy?

The decision wasn't an easy one. But Virgie and Mildred

were such good students that they'd had no trouble gaining college acceptance funded by scholarships. By this time, Virgie was attending school in Davao, and Mildred was accepted to a college in Cebu. Though I worried about Mildred moving so far away, I knew that her older half-brother, Simplicio, would look out for her. Without the older girls at home, I felt more secure about making the move. I had a serious talk with Grace—though not the first—reminding her that she must be cautious about Rudy. Even little Josephine knew it was best to steer clear of him.

In exchange for our living there, my chores at Erlinda's house increased. I did laundry, cooked their family's food, and cleaned their rooms—all this in addition to caring for my own children. I was lucky that my kids were all so intelligent, so I never had to worry about their school tuition.

In fact, the children became quite resourceful and were quick to help me whenever they could. After doing homework at night, Grace helped me with household chores, mending clothes, and cleaning, while Gary and Emmanuel helped the outdoor workers with caring for the lawns.

Over the years, we all had learned to live with the loss of Doming, often talking about our happy memories of him. Gary was an ambitious boy, focused on success, much like his father. I hoped Doming watched his son proudly from Heaven. Though ordinarily Gary kept his thoughts close to his chest, one night he spoke, saying "Mama, I'm going to work hard to get my education and be good at it. Then you won't have to worry about money anymore. You can just sit in a rocking chair and rest, and never have to wait on anybody again. I promise."

"I know you will be a great success, whatever you choose to do," I assured him. "But work is not a bad thing. I actually like to keep busy, most of the time."

Gary peered at me closely. "Keeping busy is not the same as working too hard."

He was too smart for his own good. "You're right," I said, "but I worked all my life to ensure I had what I needed. This is no different."

Grace, Gary, Emmanuel, Josephine, and I all slept in Erlinda's basement. Because there were no beds, we used floor mats. It was not a comfortable situation, but the children didn't complain. They understood that renting out the big house's rooms would bring in much-needed funds.

Emmanuel struggled with asthma, and the basement's moldy environment made his condition worse. Sometimes he struggled to breathe at night. Hearing that broke my heart, and made me even more resolved to keep saving money for our eventual escape.

At night I drew my name in the air, like I had done as a child. I chastised myself for hiding away under Doming's protection all those years. Why hadn't I learned how to have a career, or to manage the estate? I had been content, certain that God's plan for me was to be a wife to Doming and a mother to our children, and I had counted my blessings every day to have been delivered into a life more full of love and privilege than I had ever dreamed.

Sometimes when Adela visited me, we spoke about these things, and I told her how much I wished I had done more, learned more. She was sympathetic. "Doming always made it seem like everything was taken care of," she said. "Until suddenly...he is gone, and nothing is safe. For me, it was his prison sentence. For you, it was his death. And we're left to cope however we can."

I had spent most of my life on the Apostol estate and knew no other home. But I told myself, *I must get past my fear of the unknown. I must be willing to brave a bigger world.* After I saved enough money, I planned to take us all to Davao or even Cebu. The medical care there would be better. My stepchildren would help us, I felt certain. We could begin a new life in one of those places. Virgie and Mildred could soon join us. Surely that would be better than staying here, in Magpet, which had no good prospects for us.

Though I kept this to myself, I even formed an idea of taking us all to Japan, to see if I could convince that government to give me citizenship. I had no paperwork, but if I told them the story of my parents, perhaps they would accept me. The idea of absconding away to another country made my stomach ache with anxiety, yet there was also a tinge of intrigue to the idea. The biggest problem was: I spoke no Japanese. Who would understand me?

And worst of all: we would be completely on our own.

CHAPTER TWENTY

# NEVER FORGOTTEN

It was 1979. There was a ruckus in the streets of Magpet. A car from Davao had braved the terrible roads to make the trip here. Lost in my thoughts, I hardly noticed. I trudged through the humid day, eyes downcast to watch my footing as I carried a load of filled baskets toward Erlinda's home. The people of Magpet were polite to me, but I was always busy and didn't have time to chat. If they wanted to whisper and gossip about a fancy car parked in the town square, it was not my concern.

"Diamon," I heard someone say from a distance. "Hey, listen."

I moved on, lost in thought with my plans for our future.

The voice spoke again. "Diamon, Diamon, listen up! Hey, there are people here, fancy folk, parked in the town square. They want to ask you some questions."

I finally understood someone was addressing me, and I paused, finding myself looking into the face of a neighbor woman. She pointed toward the town square, where I could see a curious crowd gathered around the car from Davao.

"What's the matter?" I asked.

"It's an odd thing," she confided. "A couple of Japons—married, I think. From Davao. They have questions for you. You must go speak to them."

This stoked my curiosity. While some Filipinos had Japanese genes in their bloodline, I had never seen another full-blooded Japanese person before. The neighbor woman helped me with my burdensome baskets, and together we approached the square. The crowd parted as people realized I was there. Beside a rented car stood three people: a Filipino man and a foreign-looking couple.

The couple appeared elegant, well-dressed, and obviously married. I could tell by their body language, the familiar way they stood next to each other. I drank in their appearance with fascination. I put their age at mid-to-late forties. Their faces, shaped like mine, were kind and eager, but I could see they were tired. The three-hour trip from Davao on the rough roads had been hard on them, yet there was something else wearing them down. They were losing hope for some reason. My heart felt a pang of sadness for them.

The person with them was a translator, an older Filipino man who listened to their Japanese questions carefully and then relayed the information to me in Tagalog. He introduced me to them as Diamond Apostol.

This woman, he explained, was Mrs. Miyagi, from

Okinawa, Japan. She was here with her husband looking for information about her family. The Miyagis had already made two trips to Mindanao over the past few years. This was their third trip, and they were about to give up hope. But on this trip, in Davao, they had heard something about me: the only Japon in the town of Magpet. And they thought that I might know some useful information. They had come all the way here to ask.

"When Mrs. Miyagi was a young girl, before World War II, her parents came to the Philippines for business," explained the translator, as Mrs. Miyagi carefully told him the tale. "Mrs. Miyagi herself did not join them here, because she was old enough to stay behind in Japan, to attend school and take care of the family property. Then war struck, and they all lost contact—a terrible situation. Many families were separated this way for decades.

"The United States took control of Okinawa and kept it until 1972. When Okinawa was finally returned to Japan, the Okinawan people, at last, could begin searching for their families abroad, and thousands have done so.

"Mrs. Miyagi here is the last known survivor of her Okinawan family, and she has searched for her family for years. It has been a journey of disappointment after disappointment. Still, she has hope that you might have information about any Japanese people in the area...anything at all."

I managed to smile at the woman, who looked at me with desperate hope in her eyes. "Please tell her I am so sorry," I informed the translator. "I know of no other Japanese people.

I am the only one. I was just a child when the war began. I remember...almost nothing. She and her husband are the first Japanese people I have ever met in person."

Did I want to tell these sad people the ugly truth? If Mrs. Miyagi's family had been anywhere near here, they very likely faced the same bloody fate that mine had: murder at the hands of angry guerilla fighters. I could see how much they wanted me to give them answers.

This poor woman had been separated from her family since World War II and had been to Mindanao three times since 1972, holding onto the faith that somehow she would find her missing parents and siblings. How wonderful it would have been to help reunite them, to give her some direction to search, if only I could have told her anything of use.

Suddenly I heard the bright voice of a child. A little girl came bounding up, breaking through the crowd to join Mr. and Mrs. Miyagi. She was clearly their daughter. I heard her mother call her "Tomoko" and ask the usual motherly questions, the same no matter the language: "Where have you been? What have you been up to?"

Tomoko had been exploring the town square, it seemed. She gestured toward a few of our local places and chattered to her mother. I couldn't help but smile, because the child reminded me so much of my own girls—or what my girls could have been, with enough food and fewer worries on their young minds.

Then Mrs. Miyagi gestured to me and seemed to be explaining to little Tomoko that I was the Japanese person they had come to question.

Bright-faced, Tomoko examined me. With a look of pleased surprise, she told her parents something that made them both peer at me with sudden, intense interest. I felt myself tremble inside, as if I had been accused of something. I looked to the translator for help.

He too examined me with renewed interest. "The young miss says that you look exactly like Mrs. Miyagi's aunt, that is, the sister of Mrs. Miyagi's father, the father she now searches for."

"Koyabu," said Tomoko, pointing at me. This was the aunt's name; that much was clear.

Mrs. Miyagi approached me suddenly, gazing into my face with such scrutiny that I felt myself blush and my trembling worsen. She began to speak quickly, glancing anxiously at the translator, who had a difficult time keeping up with her.

"Ma'am, please," said the translator. "She wishes to know anything—anything at all you may remember—about your family."

Mrs. Miyagi took my hands, squeezing them. I could not refuse her.

I told the translator what I could. "I remember so little. Really I know only what the people of Magpet have told me. My parents lived in a small town nearby, but they were killed when the war began. Afterward, I was raised by villagers in the area and was finally brought to Magpet. I think I was about six years old when my parents died, but I have no papers, nothing to help. I remember...maybe...a mother, a father...I can count to ten in Japanese...but I was so small."

Mrs. Miyagi asked a quick question, and the translator repeated it to me in Tagalog. "When Mrs. Miyagi's parents came here, they brought two daughters with them, a young girl and an infant. Was there another child? Did you have a little sister?"

My stomach clenched. I closed my eyes and remembered the wails of the baby in my mother's arms. Through the years, I had sometimes wondered if I only imagined the child. "There *was*," I said. "I had a baby sister. I remember my mother holding her when the...the men with machetes came bursting in. I never saw the baby again. Never knew what happened to her."

Gripping me by the shoulders, Mrs. Miyagi gazed into my face and began to cry. Her tears were a combined torrent of abject sadness, for the loss of parents she had so hopefully sought, and for the overwhelming relief of finding *someone* after so many decades. After a moment she pulled me against her in an embrace full of love and happiness. Her husband approached, speaking excitedly, and their daughter Tomoko jumped up and down, chattering in return.

I was too astonished to react. I had the most outrageous desire to flee once again, to rush away and hide. That had always kept me safe before. But no! I was not in danger. I was not in trouble! This might be a miracle, opening up before me.

I pulled back from Mrs. Miyagi, and felt myself shaking with emotion. The crowd around us grew by the minute, but I ceased to notice them. The world shrank down to just me and this woman from Japan. I tried to tell her that perhaps this was all a mistake, but a deep surging emotion inside me wouldn't deny the possibility. Surely hundreds, even thousands of Japanese people came to the Philippines with small children before the war. Just because I remembered a baby didn't mean much...*think, Diamond, think!* Could I truly be a long-lost sibling to this woman weeping tears of joy?

Hands to my mouth, I stared into this stranger's face and concentrated as hard as possible. I'd had so many dreams through the years, of a time before the night under the bamboo floor, a time when I was surrounded by people who loved me.

Bolstered by the assurance that I had not simply dreamed that entire other life, I realized that I remembered more than just a man, a woman, and a baby. There had been others, in some distant, cool place. A vision swam up. There had been an older girl and a boy, who sat and played with me, tickled me, held me up so I could see better, helped me with my slippers, or held my hand when we went outside.

I wanted so much to connect this woman with those long-ago visions, but my mind played tricks on me. *You're just imagining things. It's not possible. In this enormous world, you belong nowhere*. Did I know her face? How desperately I wanted to know her face! *Please, please.*

Then, memories came to me, from an immeasurable time and distance. The town of Magpet faded away as I remembered the sound of a girl's laughter and the smell of the beach.

"Teruko?" I asked hesitantly, putting my hands over hers. I searched her eyes for the truth and found it there.

Mrs. Miyagi's words began to spill from her in a torrent, but one word kept repeating. "Etsuko," she sobbed. "Etsuko, Etsuko."

I *knew* this word. It was my name.

## CHAPTER TWENTY-ONE

# I BELONG

All my life, from the frightening dreams of a lonely child to the wistful musings of a tumultuous adulthood, I had longed for the moment of recognition when my real life and authentic self would be revealed.

I knew I was an outsider on this island in the Philippines. Until I became the wife of Doming Apostol, Magpet never let me forget that I was a Japon. Even when people were kind to me, it didn't matter. I was the one who was unable to forget. Insulated in the Apostol home, surrounded by the children who loved me, I felt welcome and wanted, yet my foreignness was always just a step away, threatening to take my world apart.

Now it felt like a curtain had been pulled aside, revealing a hidden world. I had a place—a bloodline family. Someone, somewhere, had missed me and come to find me, even though it had taken decades. I felt as if this might be another dream. Worse, it might be a glorious chance that cruel circumstances could demolish. When Brother Tim tried to teach me to read and write, his friendship disappeared because of changes outside my control. As when my friend Celing moved away to better fortunes, I might be left alone again. My life had held too many abrupt tragedies for me to trust fate's kindness.

But the determination of Teruko Miyagi should at once have put my fears to rest. She was unwilling to release my hands. She needed no further convincing that I was her little sister. She was prepared to take me to Japan immediately. She would have put me in the car that moment and sped away if I had allowed it. She kept searching my eyes eagerly, desperate to learn everything about me.

It took us all some time to calm down, but with the translator's help, we came to an understanding together.

"Please," Teruko said, "Can we see the place where it happened? Where our parents lived, and where you were taken, Etsuko?"

The translator answered before I could, but I had to agree with him—and our opinion was confirmed by many Magpet citizens surrounding us. Constant guerilla warfare in the region made it exceptionally dangerous. There was no way to explore safely. They told the Miyagis about my husband Doming's terrible fate on the road, and Teruko looked at me with renewed sympathy.

I told the Miyagi family, "You must come to meet my children. They will be home from school soon! They have to know about this!"

Mr. Miyagi asked, "Do your children know you are from Japan?"

To my surprise, I had to think about my answer. After a lifetime of keeping my thoughts and feelings to myself, it remained difficult to explain such things aloud. Finally, I hesitantly offered this explanation. "I do not talk about it much. They know their mama is different from the other people in Magpet. There are always rumors. Sometimes they come home from school with questions, but I only say I was orphaned young and adopted by Magpet."

So we all went together to Erlinda's house. I invited the Miyagis and the translator inside. It took me some time to explain that I had spent most of my life in the house next door, first as a maid, then as a nanny, then as the lady of the house and wife of the chief and mayor. And then, finally, I moved into this house as a widow with no resources and four children to feed.

Teruko soon understood the way of things; she looked mystified that I now worked here as my stepdaughter's maid and that my children and I slept on mats in the basement. She spoke with considerable concern to her husband. When I looked at the translator, he said, "Mrs. Miyagi says you and your children must come to live in Japan as soon as possible."

It was my second time they had told me I must come to Japan. The fact that this now was possible had not yet landed. I had fantasized for months about just such a move. Yet now, with a real opportunity, the idea seemed outlandish, impossible. For most of my life, I'd considered Japan a place like Heaven, far out of mortal reach. And if suddenly we were *invited* to Japan, I couldn't imagine what would happen after that. Even if Teruko's family came to believe, as she did, that I was one of their lost children, what would that mean? Could they help me? Would they?

Erlinda soon joined us at her house. She had heard the gossip sweeping through town. Ever attractive and intelligent, she was gracious to the Miyagis and interested in their plans for me and the children. I believe that in her own temperamental way, Erlinda was trying to protect us. As was her nature, she attempted to take charge.

Teruko and her husband discussed letting my children and me come to Japan first as tourists, to spend the maximum amount of time allowed for tourism while the family got to know us. Erlinda volunteered to join us on the journey. But Teruko was firmly set against the idea, her dark eyes fixed searchingly, accusingly, on Erlinda. It was impossible for Teruko to understand the hardships of my life, hardships that I had seldom thought to question myself. I might not have held Erlinda entirely responsible for our dire circumstances, but Teruko obviously did.

My children came home from school to meet these wondrous strangers. Tomoko and Josephine, close in age, smiled warmly and began to admire each other's hair, which made me laugh with surprise. They didn't speak each other's language and still could seem to understand. Gary and Grace shook Mr. Miyagi's hand and bowed as well. Emmanuel hung back a little, mistrustfully. "My two oldest girls are in college," I explained. "Virgie is in Davao. It should be easy for you to meet her. Mildred is far north in Cebu."

Finally a decision was made on how to proceed. The Miyagis would return to Japan and tell their Okinawan relations what they had found here, to get their opinions and input. The Miyagis took my picture. "We will show the family in Japan," they promised me. "The similarity is remarkable. They will see, and everyone will agree, that you are our lost Etsuko."

Watching the Miyagis leave was difficult. I felt as if I came out of a dream, to find myself surrounded by Magpet once more, the same life as I'd had the day before, yet with everything utterly changed. I contacted Mildred and Virgie to let them know what had happened. My two oldest daughters were overjoyed and said they could tell a difference in me, as well.

Everyone in town—I think everyone in the region—suddenly knew that a Japanese couple had claimed me as family. It was all anyone spoke about for the days that followed. When the children went to school, they were peppered with questions about their Japanese family. I continued my ordinary work life, but people from Magpet now joined me, helping out and using the chance to ask about my grand adventure.

The older children—Dodong, Orlando, Rodolfo, Rachel, Evelyn, and Sarah—were all extremely happy for me, but also concerned about what this meant for my future and that of their younger half-siblings. They wanted assurance that, if the children and I went to Japan, we would have the means to support ourselves and adjust to a strange new place.

In November of 1979, Teruko and her husband, whose

name was Hideshin, returned to us. Apparently they wanted to waste no time. They came back to Magpet, their rented car loaded with gifts, treats, and clothing for us all. The translator came again as well, but to my amazement, I was already beginning to understand many of the things Teruko said. I wondered if the language had been hiding in the back of my mind, waiting to be uncovered a bit at a time.

Teruko told me that the family in Okinawa was almost 100% convinced that I was Etsuko. They all agreed with Teruko's original desire: that I must visit them in Okinawa.

On this, their fourth visit to the Philippines, the Miyagis stayed in Davao for two weeks while traveling back and forth to update me on the progress with the paperwork that would allow me to come to Japan. They enjoyed meeting Virgie, who escorted them around Davao and showed them the many places we used to go as a family. It seemed at first that the easiest thing, as far as the bureaucracy of paperwork was concerned, would be for me to visit Japan alone.

I was elated at this blessing of finding my family, this gift from God. But I knew better than to think I could leave Magpet without my children. A lifetime of experience had taught me that much. What's more, I could not leave Grace or even little Josephine in Erlinda's home without my supervision. I would never trust Rudy again.

"No," I told Teruko. "Please understand, I want so badly to come. Virgie and Mildred should finish their college here, and they are nearly grown women who can do without me for a little while. But I will not leave my four youngest behind. If I go to Japan, they must come too. There is no other way."

"Of course," she agreed. "You have suffered enough. We

will make this happen. Nothing will stop us!"

Before the end of that month, I and my youngest children—Grace, Gary, Emmanuel, and Josephine—arrived in Okinawa. The Japanese government granted us all a three-month visa. The children would be permitted to join local public schools as exchange students. After three months, we could return home to the Philippines if we wanted to.

My children were as worried as they were hopeful. The prospect of a new life in Japan thrilled them, but naturally they fretted about leaving their friends and school behind. Grace, who was a senior in high school in the Philippines, went from anxiety to excitement about the adventure of it all. Gary, an eighth grader, worried about fitting in. "What if they don't like Filipinos in Japan?" Emmanuel, in fourth grade, repeatedly fretted, "I can't make friends if I can't speak Japanese!" And Josephine, in third grade, agreed, asking "How will we talk to anyone?"

"It will be alright," I assured them all. "Don't be afraid. We will be with family—with each other, and with the Miyagis, too."

Taking my first deep breath of air in Japan, I felt such sheer amazement. The faces that surrounded us looked familiar. The sound of the Japanese voices gave me deep comfort. My children stood around me, huddled close—curious, nervous, but not afraid, because they could see that I stood straighter and happier than ever before.

## CHAPTER TWENTY-TWO

# GUESTS IN A NEW WORLD

We created quite a stir in the village of Kitanakagusuku, the Miyagis' home town. Naturally, Teruko and her husband had told everyone weeks ago that I had been found, and people went to considerable trouble to come and wish us well and to sate their curiosity. Unaccustomed to this level of attention, I felt as shy as I had when I was a child under scrutiny. Excited conversations chattered around us that we did not understand, though Teruko, Hideshin, and Tomoko tried their best to include us.

Love, patience, and curiosity definitely aided in our two families getting to know each other. We developed a sort of basic vocabulary for everyday things so that we could ask for what we needed, yet sometimes I had to laugh at the bothersome truth that we could only communicate in the simplest of terms. Teruko had a little translation book, but her attempts at Tagalog often had the whole family laughing together.

The people could not have been kinder, despite our inability to speak their language. Josephine picked up Japanese faster than any of us; she was soon able to have simple conversations with other children. Sometimes she was able to translate for me, or read signs and labels to me.

The Miyagi family ran a quaint mom-and-pop grocery shop nestled in the front section of their home. In the afternoons following their school day, Grace and Gary, the two older siblings, alternated responsibilities managing the store. This routine not only anchored them within the community but also served as a lively language lab where they honed their Japanese-speaking skills through engaging conversations with the locals. Both siblings found deep enjoyment in this enriching experience.

The Miyagis' relations did something wondrous: they accepted us as family members without question, and spoiled us with little gifts and surprises. They were eager to take us everywhere, to show us everything. Our knowledge of Japan was minimal; the children had learned only general knowledge in school. The culture and everyday life of the country were entirely new. Our newfound family and friends took great pleasure in introducing us to their lifestyle, and I believe it made them rediscover their good fortune to live in such a safe and modern place.

Throughout our visit, we saw delicate Shinto shrines, where Japanese gods were honored with incense and rice. Teruko had a similar shrine for our parents, though she had always held onto the distant hope that they were alive in the Philippines. I marveled at the photographs. In my mother's face, I saw my own; in my father's face, I saw hints of Gary and Emmanuel slipping through, despite their strong resemblance to Doming. How amazing this was!

Teruko had told me that Kitanakagusuku was a "village" but it was about five times the size of Magpet. Fortunately I had been to Davao enough times that a bustling town did not unnerve me. Everything here was clean and well cared for, not subject to the ravages of downpours, excessive humidity, muddy dirt roads, or encroaching jungle.

The children and I had to adjust to sleeping with the sounds of a town around us, though I soon found that nights without fear of nearby gunfire were a blessing. I drilled Emmanuel and Josephine on taking care when crossing streets, because after a few hesitant days, they itched to get out and look around. The polite, curious neighborhood children were more than happy to oblige and act as tour guides.

Our November arrival put us in the late fall season, with Okinawa's winter just around the corner. The climate was cool and dry. For the first few weeks, my children and I were chilled to the bone. We bundled up in sweaters, clutching our hands together, needing extra covers at night. I had never experienced weather this cold, though Teruko told me this was mild compared to the winters further north. She communicated this by pointing to Kitanakagusuku on a map and pretending to shiver, then pointing to the cities in the north and pretending to shiver violently, her teeth chattering and her shoulders hunched protectively. I understood her meaning at once, and we had a good laugh together. Laughing once more with my sister reminded me of the phrase Brother Tim had taught me: this was one of "life's great pleasures."

Kitanakagusuku was considerably more advanced than Magpet, with good roads and reliable utilities. Sometimes I felt like a time traveler who had slipped a few decades into the future. We were able to take Emmanuel to a spotless, quiet doctor's office for more effective asthma treatment. There were dentists in town all the time, not just on certain days of the month or in faraway city offices. When we walked through the Miyagis' little shop or the other grocery stores, my children exchanged looks, marveling, for while the shopping in Kitanakagusuku was not elaborate, we had never seen so many brand names, so much colorful packaging, so many magazines, and such an ease of availability.

Every home had a telephone, and the phones were never disrupted by storms or downed lines. There seemed to be hundreds of cars, with law enforcement officers on street corners. The firefighters fascinated Emmanuel. We saw a lending library, uniformed mail carriers, and public parks. There were so many people doing specific jobs. "Who is that?" Emmanuel would ask Tomoko. "What is she doing? Does she do that every day? How did she learn?"

I was struck by the variety of jobs and by the level of education everyone seemed to have. As introductions were made and Teruko explained to me what these people did, I was constantly amazed. The women were as educated as the men, some of them more so. They did jobs I had never even thought about women doing. I met women of all walks of life, those who were teachers, doctors, musicians, shop owners, newspaper reporters, tailors, homemakers, architects, and photographers. Many of them told me they also had children, and it was considered normal for a woman to have both a family and a job. When I mentioned, in a phone call with Virgie, how much this surprised me, she said, "Mama, you worked more jobs than anyone. You just didn't get a paycheck for it."

Even homes were different, in their design, materials, and furniture. We were surprised at how much Japanese home life was spent on the floor, on small cushions rather than chairs, and on soft mats rather than beds. We adjusted to meals served at low tables, with our legs tucked neatly beneath us. Dining from a seated position on the floor is actually good for the posture and digestion, I learned later, but this was not an easy switch to make. We were clumsy at first in managing it, and a great deal of food was dropped on laps and on the floor. The Miyagis were endlessly patient with us, and we all had a sense of humor about it.

The Miyagis had things in their home that were delightful discoveries, like kitchen appliances and clock radios, and many little gadgets I'd never seen before. The television set was a marvel that the children couldn't get enough of, sitting before it with a hand on the knob as they turned through the channels. Hideshin warned them not to sit too close, but there was a hint of humor in his eyes when he said it. I think he enjoyed their fascination.

I observed that Hideshin greeted each dawn and dusk with equal reverence, sitting before the television to catch the day's headlines. With a steaming plate of food, he attentively absorbed the world's stories, narrated by familiar faces of newscasters. In an endearing display of sincerity, he would nod in thoughtful acknowledgement, returning their televised greetings with a gentle bow and a warm, spoken salutation.

As happy as I felt, my adjustment to this world was often challenging. I contended not only with a new environment, but with a new identity, one which left me with an unusual amount of privilege. Not even as Diamond Apostol had I ever felt so constantly doted upon. I had but to smile at some object, and someone would give it to me or get me one just like it. I needed only to look curiously at some machine and they would gladly show me how it worked, demonstrating in detail and offering to let me try. As someone who was never comfortable being the center of attention, this tired me out quickly, and Teruko or Hideshin often had to shoo people away so that I could have some peace. To the town, my children and I were still a novelty.

One thing I rather liked was that Japanese body language was more reserved and deferential than what I was accustomed to. They did not stand too close together when speaking, and kept their manners more formal. Teruko told me that body language is different in almost all cultures, and I had to admit I'd never even thought about that. I wondered if I had learned the Japanese mannerisms as a small child, carrying that tendency with me all these years, making me always shy away from public displays of hugging, arms slung around shoulders, and heads close together when people spoke.

While I had my challenges, my children were the ones who had to make the most obvious and sometimes upsetting changes. We were there on a three-month visa, and Teruko arranged for all four of them to attend school. Since they spoke no Japanese, they had to be reassigned in their grades. They had always been the top performers in their classes and were accustomed to outshining the other students.

Grace, who had been a high school senior in the Philippines, was reentered as a freshman and treated like a foreign exchange student. She coped fairly well with this, especially with Tomoko's guidance and encouragement. She was a pretty young woman, and her Filipino heritage gave her a slightly exotic look compared to the other girls, so she soon had several shy admirers offering to help her with schoolwork or share a bench at lunchtime.

Gary, though, who had been an eighth grader in the Philippines, was put all the way back into first-grade-level instruction. This was extremely difficult for him to deal with. Naturally he did not have to do recess and activities with the first graders, but he had their simple primers and assignments, and I could see it irked him to feel like he was starting over. He was accustomed to being the smartest, quickest learner in his grade, and now he struggled with simple grammar lessons. The childish books he was given to study embarrassed him; he kept them out of sight except when doing his homework.

And as for that homework, he, Josephine, and Emmanuel

all worked together, for their assignments were almost exactly the same. Emmanuel and Josephine also had to go back to first grade. Their adjustment was quicker than Gary's, though. They were both young enough that their minds could make the switch more easily, and they didn't feel as out of place or embarrassed as Gary did about their "demotion" back to the beginning.

We were fortunate in that the Japanese children at school were fascinated with my kids and accepted them warmly. Word had gotten around of my life's strange adventure, so it seemed that everyone in town was happy to have us returned to them, even if my children were half Filipino.

The children suffered no ill treatment, although it was hard to believe from the way Emmanuel and Josephine complained when returning home from school. Oh, they enjoyed the other students, their classes, and their teachers, but the school lunches were "weird" and "strange." Japanese cuisine was quite a switch for us all, but children are notoriously picky about eating sometimes. Finding anything the little ones would willingly eat was a daily experiment, though thankfully they found plain rice inoffensive enough, and they liked learning to use chopsticks.

All in all, we enjoyed an amazing adventure. But our three-month visa passed, and soon enough it was time to decide what we wanted to do. We could return to the Philippines or extend the visa for more time in Japan. The Miyagis wanted for us to stay; they said as much, telling us we were a welcome part of their home. There was so much more to see and do here, they explained, showing us pictures of the places they wanted to take us. I could see Teruko's concern that she might be separated from me once more. I hated the thought of that, too, yet adjusting to living in Japan had already been rather exhausting, and I wasn't sure we could continue like this.

As overjoyed as I was to have found my family, and as much as I loved Teruko and her family, I was uncertain about staying. Japan was wonderful, it was true. Yet the Philippines beckoned with its familiarity. Most of my beloved stepchildren were there, as well as my friends in Magpet. That was a life I knew, and a language I could speak. Though I had never been a talkative person, I was surprised at how I longed to have an easy conversation with another adult, to be able to just talk about something without thinking through which words to use. The inability to speak well left me feeling rather lonely. I felt a strong pull to go home.

I gathered my children together for a serious discussion. Grace, Gary, Emmanuel, and Josephine joined me around the Miyagis' table, where we knelt in the style we had learned, our knees bent and legs folded beneath us.

"We must decide what we want to do," I told the kids. "We can return to our home in Magpet. Don't worry; it wouldn't mean parting ways with our new family. The Miyagis could visit us there whenever they wanted to, and we could visit here as well. I miss our home, but I want to hear what you all think."

"I miss my school friends," said Emmanuel.

Josephine agreed. "I miss my teacher. I don't like the food here. It's weird."

"I want to return to my own grade," Gary said. "This business with starting over is torture."

"Torture!" exclaimed my oldest daughter. "Aren't you being a little dramatic? No one is making you have naptime with the toddlers."

"Easy for you to say," Gary said. "They didn't send you all the way back to first grade. This is impossible. I'll be twenty-eight before I get done with high school. This could really hurt my chances of getting into college."

"I do miss the familiar surroundings," I said. "I haven't got much to do here, and I'm restless. And it would be nice to feel warm again..."

Grace intervened once more. "Listen, my dears," she said to her siblings. "Listen, Mama," she said to me. When she had our full attention, she explained, "I'm homesick for some things, too. I had many friends in Magpet, and learning Japanese isn't easy, and I know the food is odd and everything is different here. Being homesick is making us only remember the good things, though.

"Emmanuel, remember how sick you felt with your asthma? It's much better here, isn't it? Mama, do you want to go back to doing other people's laundry in the river? Don't any of you remember how hard Mama had to work day and night for us just to make certain we had food and clothes? Do you want to return to sleeping in Erlinda's basement? Gary, only last year, you told me that you wanted nothing more than to have a career so that Mama wouldn't have to work another day."

"Things would be better at home now," Gary argued,

but he looked a shade guilty. “The Miyagis will help us. We won’t be so poor.”

“I mean no disrespect for our friends in Magpet,” Grace said, “but that region isn’t always safe. Papa was murdered before Josephine even got a chance to know him well, and no one was ever brought to justice for it. Japan is a modern country that is moving forward fast. Our opportunities here are ten times better. We mustn’t be afraid. All we must do is learn a little more Japanese, and we’ll be able to do anything.”

We exchanged uncertain glances, even as I felt a rush of pride for Grace’s courage and sense of adventure. She could tell her arguments were good ones and that she had us reconsidering.

Now she spoke urgently. “Let’s make a compromise. Let’s extend our visa and stay one more year, and see how we feel then. If we are still homesick and struggling then, I will agree that we should return to the Philippines.”

CHAPTER TWENTY-THREE

# CITIZENS OF JAPAN

We agreed to stay through the year, much to the delight of the Miyagis. For a little while our homesickness got a bit worse, and the language seemed harder than ever. But somewhere around our fifth month in Japan, things began to normalize. We were no longer the center of attention everywhere we went. My children made new friends, and I marveled at hearing little Josephine chatting away in Japanese to the girls she walked home from school with, or watching Emmanuel and her dash off to play baseball in the park with the other neighborhood children. I had no need to worry about their safety. Hours later they'd return, grubby, with glowing cheeks.

Gary, who'd felt the pressure of switching schools more than his siblings, had a turnaround, and was able to start moving quickly through school material. When it came time for the new school year, he was moved up to fifth-grade level learning, and I could see that this was a tremendous relief to him. He'd feared doing elementary school over again from start to finish!

Grace wanted to stay in Okinawa more than any of us, and proved it by applying herself fiercely to her school work. Her Aunt Teruko hired a language tutor for her, so Grace would be sure to pass her college entrance exams when the time came.

Meanwhile, Teruko applied to have my Japanese citizenship reinstated. The process went smoothly. My name was given back to me: I could officially identify myself as Etsuko Miyagi. As a Japanese citizen, I no longer needed a visa to remain. I could stay for the rest of my life in the country of my birth, along with my children, if that was what I wanted.

One year became two, then three. Five years later, we were still in Okinawa. My children got their Japanese citizenship. Once we decided to stay, the Miyagis had a little house built for us on one of their properties. Our parents had owned several parcels of land in Okinawa, which had been left to Teruko's supervision when they went to the Philippines before World War II.

When we moved into the little house, I understood it was time for me to make a place for myself in this fascinating country. Because I was a single parent, I received financial assistance from the government. I had also taken a job working at the nearby chrysanthemum farm as a flower harvester. The feeling of receiving a paycheck—a first-time experience for me—was amazing. I was so happy, earning money for my family.

I learned quickly that chrysanthemums are quite an important flower to the Japanese. Images of the flower are often found in traditional clothing and paintings. There is even a chrysanthemum depicted on a Japanese coin. They are flowers of nobility, and a symbol of the Japanese emperor. Red chrysanthemums are given as gifts of respect and love, while white chrysanthemums are for mourning, used for funerals and placed on graves. Colorful chrysanthemums are used in bonsai art. Moving through the fragrant flowers with their bright balls of ruffly petals, gathering those that were ready to be sold, I felt ever more connected to the land of my birth.

Protective as always, Teruko observed the job with consternation. "Etsuko, it's such hard work! Outside all day, bent over, working your hands raw!"

She was correct; the job was not easy work. But compared with years of toiling over a Magpet farm in the heat and humidity, in exchange for almost nothing but a little food, this was a pleasure. With my improving Japanese, I explained to her, "I like to work outdoors, and I'm used to it. If I don't work, I go crazy with boredom!"

"Yes, I've seen that," she replied with a smile. She knew very well how I tended to go looking for chores if I needed something to occupy my time.

"Also," I confessed, "the flowers don't speak, so I don't

have to worry about my poor Japanese."

"You're getting better every day," said Teruko.

Our family found an American-missionary-led Baptist church in Okinawa, and we became active members. There Gary and Grace made friends and could practice speaking English, a language they had begun to study in the Philippines. Emmanuel and Josephine were always more comfortable speaking in Japanese.

My work at the chrysanthemum farm did not go unnoticed—apparently I was an enthusiastic and hardworking employee. The manager of a famous tourist attraction in the area was impressed with my efforts. She offered me a job as caretaker for the plants and grounds of Nakamura Residence, a nationally recognized piece of Japanese history.

This peaceful, elegant house—built in the eighteenth century for the Nakamura family—sat surrounded by tall trees and guarded from evil spirits by statues of fierce shisa. There was a constant stream of visitors. Often I saw couples in traditional Japanese dress, having their wedding photographs taken. It was an absolutely beautiful place to work.

There I made some good friends, and my boss was extremely kind and generous. Each day I walked to work because the site was so close to home. My salary was good enough that I could often send money to Virgie and Mildred. This was a wonderful feeling, harkening back to the days when I was married to Doming and could afford to be generous with my friends. I would continue to work there until I retired.

I have little to regret. I could not ask for a more wonderful family. After Doming's death, whether in the Philippines or Japan, I never considered remarrying. Marriage to Doming had been enough: often wonderful, yet sometimes heartbreaking. I did not want to live with a second husband and lose my independence, nor did I think anyone could compare to Doming when he had been at his best. I always carried him in my heart as the father of my children and the man who sheltered me and gave me a life I had never expected.

After graduating from college in Davao with a bachelor's degree in civil engineering, Virgie passed the national licensing board exam. She then moved to Japan to join us in the later part of 1983. Mildred followed in 1984 after she finished her bachelor's in industrial engineering.

I was thrilled to have all of us together under one roof once more. We spoke a dizzying mix of languages in the house, the language shifting depending on who we were speaking to. The younger children communicated in Japanese among themselves and to me, while my oldest two girls spoke only in our Filipino dialect. Virgie and Mildred often needed Gary or Grace to translate when they spoke to Emmanuel or Josephine. Gary and Grace spoke in English to their American friends, adding a third language to the household.

A kind neighbor, Mr. Higa, assisted Virgie and Mildred in getting jobs with local architect and engineering firms. In an amazing stroke of luck, these jobs provided services to United States military bases. Fluency in Japanese was not required, and the girls had learned a great deal of English in the Philippines.

Imagine how proud I was to see my daughters working in positions where they could use their sharp intelligence and skills. I thanked God that they would never again need to feel the sting of poverty in their lives. They even helped out with household expenses and in sending their younger siblings through college. All of my children were acutely aware of the importance of a good education; it was something their father had always emphasized. They would never forget how he had celebrated their academic successes.

While all this was happening, Gary made incredible progress in school. He began junior high only a year behind his normal class level, and by senior high he was even with other students his age. Gary decided years before that he wanted to be a doctor, and for a while he feared his struggles with Japanese would make that difficult or even impossible in Japan.

He need not have feared, not as hard as he worked. He passed the medical entrance test for Ryukyu University School of Medicine, which was a national college. Gary was the first student from Kitanagusuku High School to pass this test, and as such was featured in an article in the *Okinawa Times*.

The years flew by in a series of peaceful days and joyous

family events. In 1987, Mildred married a young American and in 1989 moved to the United States, where she continued her career in engineering. We all hated to see Mildred and her husband move so far away, but we were so proud of her that we could hardly be sad.

Meanwhile, Virgie had married her college sweetheart in 1988. They remained in Okinawa and flourished in their engineering careers.

Grace moved to mainland Japan to attend a Christian missionary college while working as a part-time secretary for an American missionary. In 1992 she was married in Kobe to a wonderful man from Croatia.

Gary thrived in medical school. He received many scholarship offers from large companies and became a successful doctor.

Following high school, Emmanuel's entrepreneurial spirit led him to try the wholesale produce business. In 1999 he built his own home, but he remained a bachelor.

Finally, my youngest, Josephine, achieved a degree in interior design and married her local sweetheart.

During those years, something unexpected happened, which I am so glad to be able to share. Erlinda, Doming's oldest daughter, was one of my life's great enigmas. For some time after the children and I went to Japan, Mildred remembers staying in Erlinda's house whenever she returned to Magpet for weekend visits from college. Once Mildred encountered Erlinda in the basement, where Erlinda was folding some of Josephine's left-behind clothing. There were tears on Erlinda's face. It seemed to Mildred that Erlinda really did miss us in her own way.

In 1989, Erlinda visited us in Okinawa. I was nervous about her coming, for many reasons. We had such a long, strange history together. But she came with an open heart and an open mind, much to my delight. Our family gave her a tour of Okinawa's beauties and enjoyed introducing her to Japanese cuisine.

Throughout, I could tell that she was eager to ease some burden in herself. I believe this happens to everyone at a certain time in their lives; we become wise enough to see where we went wrong, and if we're lucky, there is still time to make amends.

Though it was difficult to catch her alone during that busy, exciting visit, I did manage to have a quiet breakfast with Erlinda one day. I was no longer intimidated by her, thankfully, and was able to say, "I'm glad you came to visit, Erlinda. I think this was good for all of us."

She looked relieved. "I was nervous about asking to visit. I'm grateful that you allowed me to come. I missed the children, and..." She considered her next words, then looked at me frankly. "I've never been very kind to you. I know that."

"Well," I said thoughtfully. "You were never *very* kind to anybody."

For a moment she looked at me, then realized I was teasing her. "No," she agreed with a hearty laugh. "No, you're right. I'm difficult. My parents were difficult people, and I dealt with their problems from the time I was a child. And then I grew up to behave exactly like them."

"I always saw how hard it was for you," I said. "I secretly admired your confidence and intelligence, and sometimes wished I could be more like you."

"Diamond," she began, then corrected herself. "Etsuko, I mean. Yes, you always saw everything. I don't know if I can make amends for all of your hardships, but I am truly happy for you now. Finding your Japanese family was a miracle."

"It was," I agreed. "But it does not change who I am inside. The Apostol family—all of us—will always be my heart's greatest love."

Others joined us then, and so we spoke no further about it. Yet nothing more needed to be said. Holding on to anger or regret is pointless. When Erlinda returned to the Philippines, I gave her a sincere embrace and wished her all the best.

I had an astonishing adventure in 1996, one that I still enjoy remembering. I share the stories again and again.

I traveled to the United States to be with Mildred when she delivered her first baby. My excitement was almost too much to handle. My friends said things to me like, "I can't believe you're going! You're so brave! You don't even speak the language!" But they forgot, this would not be the first time I accepted an invitation to another country despite knowing little about it. And it takes less bravery to board an airplane than to cross a dangerous jungle in the middle of the night.

The trip was carefully planned. I met with my stepdaughter Rachel and her son Paul in Tokyo. Together, we traveled to Saint Louis, Missouri. The experience felt like a dream. American culture was different from anything I had seen before: bright, loud, forward, and full of cheer. I studied everything I saw in detail, so that I would never forget.

Rachel had been to the United States before. "The first time I was here, the trees were all bare," she told me. "I thought there had been a terrible fire. But my husband said it was autumn, and the leaves had fallen to the ground. This happened every year! Nothing like that happens in Magpet, does it?"

The highlight of the trip, of course, was the joy of holding my new grandson William, and seeing Mildred's happiness. There is nothing more exciting than the start of a new life.

EPILOGUE

# ALL THE LIVES WE TOUCH

Over the years, I returned to Magpet three times for visits. Magpet and its people will always be important to me, yet I never regretted our decision to remain in Japan.

I never lost contact with my stepchildren, all of whom I love as my own. Let me share with you the many things that have happened to my family and friends in the years that followed. I hope you'll forgive me for being exceedingly proud of them all.

**Adela**

Unknown to Doming, Adela had returned to live in Magpet in 1972, living a mere ten miles from the Apostol household. Perhaps Doming was the only one who did not know this; everyone else was aware, but no one quite dared to tell him about his ex-wife's return. My daughter Mildred actually believes Doming was aware of Adela's presence, but was content in his marriage to me, and therefore left Adela to live her own life.

After Doming's death, Adela came out of hiding. She frequently visited the town and came by the Apostol residence to chat with me. As a child I was in awe of this magnificent lady; how strange and wonderful that in later years, she and I became friends. We shared an unusual bond: not just through our strong link to Doming, but as two women who had learned to live with grief and loneliness.

Except for Sarah, Adela's children showed no interest in reforming their relationship with her. Evelyn and Rachel always considered me to be their mother. Sometimes I gently suggested that Adela was nearby and that forgiveness, while difficult, can be a pathway to new happiness. But I also knew better than to push.

Adela passed away in 1982, after a bout with cancer.

### The Miyagi Family

Through the years, Teruko Miyagi's love and support for me never wavered. She took it upon herself to teach me the ways of Japanese culture, knowing full well the challenges I faced in that foreign land. She stood firmly by my side throughout the challenging transition, offering words of encouragement and hope.

Teruko's husband, Hideshin, played a pivotal role in my life. As a father figure, he imparted valuable life lessons to my children and lent them a listening ear when they needed to vent or seek advice. He also fiercely defended my children against bullies and stood up for them when others tried to put them down.

Hideshin's untimely death in 2014 was a tremendous loss for us all, but his legacy lives on in the love and the bonds that he forged.

My beloved niece Tomoko, the Miyagis' only child, was the apple of her parents' eyes. She grew up to be a kindhearted and compassionate nurse, who doted on her parents and cared for them in their old age.

### Simplicio

Doming and Inday's son, Simplicio, passed away in 2021. He was hardworking, and dedicated to his practice as a lawyer affiliated with the Bureau of Customs in Cebu City. His commitment to his profession was evident in his successful career, and it was no surprise that his three children were equally accomplished in their chosen fields. Simplicio's daughter spent most of her professional life as a registered nurse in the city of Chicago. Another of Simplicio's children is a licensed architect in Cebu City, and the youngest owns a successful dental practice in Cebu.

You may recall that Simplicio once offered to take Mildred in and raise her as his own daughter. They always had a strong bond, and Mildred ever after felt connected to his children. Her summers spent with them are some of her fondest memories. She admired how they each pursued their dreams, contributed to society, and maintained a strong connection to their family roots.

**Erlinda**

I was fortunate that Erlinda and I had the chance to set things right between us. I am sorry to say that her family life in the Philippines was riddled with tragedy. Rudy, her husband, suffered a heart attack in 1986, which left him unable to work. He died in 2007.

Erlinda's sons were caught in the crosshairs of fate. One son died young, his body ravaged by alcoholism. Another son was deeply involved in drugs and eventually ended up in prison. The young man's addiction had gotten the better of him, and he passed away due to heart failure while incarcerated. My heart ached for Erlinda and for her boys, who had been raised alongside my own children, and for whom I had great affection. I often wished I could be there to help Erlinda cope with these terrible losses.

After a lengthy struggle with gallbladder cancer, Erlinda passed away in 2021.

**Dodong**

My oldest stepson, Dodong, enjoyed his youthful dream of being a sailor as first mate on a cargo ship. After returning home, he married a beautiful midwife from a neighboring town.

Dodong's family thrived in the small town of Magpet. His youngest daughter established herself as a highly respected medical doctor. Her dedication to her work and her patients was unparalleled, and her reputation as a kind and compassionate doctor spread far beyond the borders of the town. His other daughter carved her own successful path in the hospitality industry. She is the proud owner of a stunning resort in the now progressive town of Magpet.

Dodong went on to serve in the government as director of the National Commission of Indigenous People, acting as a mediator between the Bagobo tribes and the Philippine government. He died in 2011. The entire family grieved his loss, but celebrated his wonderful life.

**Orlando**

Orlando was a man of few words. Growing up, he was always the introverted type, and this never changed, but he was fond of women and had an impressive string of relationships. Following Doming's death, he grew more serious and took a fulltime job.

After some years of working as a bank clerk in Davao City, Orlando moved back to his hometown of Magpet and married a local beauty. Orlando's four boys, who were completely different from Orlando himself, were all adventurous and had a deep desire to explore the world and better their future in foreign countries.

Orlando served as a police officer in Magpet before he passed away in 2014. Again, we took pride in his accomplishments even as we mourned him.

**Rodolfo**

Rodolfo was a man of simplicity. He found pleasure in the quiet life provided by his humble abode in Magpet. He derived great satisfaction from farming the land passed on to him by his father, Doming.

It was not until later in life that Rodolfo married his local sweetheart. Together they raised a family of three children.

Rodolfo died in 2002. Sadly, one of my three return visits to Magpet was to attend his funeral. As I looked on his still body, I did not see his quiet form lying before me, but instead, the worried little boy he had once been, clinging to my skirt. He had been so afraid that I would leave them alone, as their mother had, and would hardly let me out of his sight. I tried my very best to always be a steady, loving presence in his life. He and Rachel were the first people in the family to truly love me, and they will forever hold that special place in my thoughts and in my heart.

I was very glad that as an adult, Rodolfo found happiness with a family of his own.

**Rachel**

Our dear Rachel, one of the most loving people I have ever known, visited us in Okinawa several times. As you know, she took me to Saint Louis in the United States to visit Mildred, giving me an unforgettable adventure.

Ever passionate about helping others, Rachel obtained a pharmacy degree and planned on making a difference in the world. Then, when she joined Campus Crusade for Christ, it was like all the pieces fell into place for her. She found a community of likeminded people who shared her faith and her passion for service. It was there that she met the man from Asheville, North Carolina, who would become her husband. They raised three sons, two of whom grew up to be missionaries themselves.

One of the greatest joys of Rachel's life was her relationship with her husband's parents and siblings. They were kind, loving people, who welcomed her into their family with great warmth. For Rachel, who had been abandoned by her own mother at a young age, their love was a powerful balm to the heart. She cherished every moment she spent with them.

In 2019, Rachel joined her brothers in Heaven.

**Evelyn**

Evelyn married a local man from Cabanatuan City, Philippines. They are blessed with one child. Evelyn was passionate about her work as a nurse and spent several years in the Middle East as a contract nurse. Since retiring from her career, she busies herself taking care of what remains of Doming Apostol's estate. Evelyn remains close to her younger siblings and maintains contact with them through email and phone calls.

**Sarah**

After Sarah married her high school sweetheart, they built a life in Davao City and raised five daughters. Sarah is proud that her daughters have all become successful professionals, with two of them now living in the U.S. and married to Americans. Sarah maintains regular contact with all of her children.

**Virgie**

My oldest daughter, Virgie, had two beautiful children with her husband. Though Virgie enjoyed and was successful in her work, her heart's desire was to spend more time with her children, and this led her to become a teacher at a Christian school. Her elder child is a talented musician and a thriving schoolteacher as well. Her younger son graduated with a master's degree in computer engineering from Texas A&M University and now works as a talented systems design engineer for one of the biggest companies in Silicon Valley.

**Mildred**

In addition to her engineering degree, Mildred holds a master's in information management from the prestigious University of Southern California. Her oldest son worked briefly in investment banking in New York City, then decided to change his career to nursing, which he thinks is his calling. Mildred's younger son is a medical doctor in Virginia and recently married his beautiful bride, who is also a doctor.

It was Mildred who took charge of ensuring that my story get published, encouraging me to share my life with the world. I would not have accomplished this without her enthusiasm and encouragement.

**Grace**

Grace is fluent in Japanese, English, Tagalog, and Bisaya. After completing her education at Kansai Independent Baptist Bible School in Japan, she spent four fruitful years as the institution's secretary and interpreter. Not content to rest on her laurels, Grace also lent a hand to American Christian missionaries who needed assistance in the area.

In 1992 Grace married an incredible man from Croatia.

Together they owned and operated a children's daycare business in bustling Takarazuka City, Hyogo Prefecture, Japan, where they built a life and raised their two beloved daughters and a cherished son. She and her family lived in the lovely country of Croatia before returning to Okinawa, Japan in 2005. With her impressive linguistic skills and infectious can-do attitude, Grace is loved and appreciated wherever she goes.

**Gary**

Like Grace, Gary speaks and writes fluent Japanese, English, Tagalog, and Bisaya.

He became a doctor, as he wished. Long ago he had promised me that one day he would earn enough that I could sit in a rocking chair all day and never work again. As I told him then, I had no desire to sit all day, but had no doubt he would be a great success. He was fully true to his word, however, and was happy to provide me with anything I ever needed.

Gary is married to a brilliant nurse who serves alongside him. His older daughter also serves as a nurse at a local Okinawa hospital, while his younger child pursues her lifelong dream of becoming a medical doctor, like her father.

**Emmanuel**

Emmanuel was the child with whom I was pregnant when I fled from Doming, the baby I carried within me as I crossed the rivers and blade grass of the jungle. And he was the baby born soon after we began to rebuild our marriage.

Doming and I always considered Emmanuel to be our symbol of forgiveness. Emmanuel's happy life is a testament to the power of faith, and the bond between a mother and her child.

Emmanuel lives in Okinawa and runs his own business. He remains steadfastly single. Today I live with Emmanuel in his home, where he is my constant caregiver and companion. Another of my life's many strange turns is that Emmanuel and I now live as I imagined we would had I never returned to Doming: just the two of us, relying on each other.

However, I am much happier that our shared life turned out this way.

### Josephine

My youngest, Josephine, was just a baby when her father, Doming, passed away. But despite her not remembering him personally, his legacy lives on through her every day, in her intelligence, bravery, and spirit.

Today Josephine is happily married to a native of Okinawa and is the proud mother of two amazing children, the older of whom is well on her way to becoming an educator.

### The Apostol Estate

Once the children and I vacated the Apostol house, we turned part of it into a boarding house for students. But that didn't last long, as the house quickly became dilapidated and was left to rot for years. Even though it had the potential for restoration to become a museum of Bagobo artifacts, those plans were halted. In early 2023, Evelyn made the executive decision to have the house demolished. The only thing that remained standing were two massive concrete vaults.

The contents of these vaults are mysterious and intriguing. Nobody knows what they hold, not even those who remember life during Doming's time and after. Evelyn sought out professional demolitionists to aid in uncovering the mystery within these concrete encasements, but the vaults were found to extend fifteen meters below the ground's surface.

There were countless rumors through the years about what Doming may have hidden in the basement—from Japanese artifacts to treasure and ammunition. The discovery of the concrete vaults reignited those rumors. Despite keen interest, further investigation was halted when unknown poisonous substances were found surrounding the boxes.

As of this writing (early 2024), Evelyn is actively working with experienced professionals to devise a safe and effective approach to unraveling these fascinating, yet bizarre encasements.

**Myself**

In 1986, scientists discovered how to test and compare DNA. Soon the technique was being used all over the world in criminal justice and for identification. Understandably, there was some talk among our relatives that Teruko and I should be tested to ensure that we were truly sisters.

My niece Tomoko had her say about this. "There is no point in taking the tests. We were the ones who invited her to come to Okinawa. After meeting her, we were convinced that she is Etsuko Miyagi. We persuaded her to stay in Okinawa even though she wanted to go back to the Philippines. She tried her best, working hard to blend in and stand on her own. As for the children, they worked hard to learn Japanese, graduated schools with flying colors, and all have successful careers. We don't need any DNA tests."

Tomoko's words rang true, and the Miyagi family stood united in their love and support for me, a bond that doubts or suspicions could never break.

I will always be grateful to God and to my family—every member, everywhere, including the mother and father I never had a chance to know. Without faith and love, I would not have survived.

I am eighty-five years old now, and some days I feel my age, the soft stirrings as my heart winds down. As is true of anyone who lives such a fine, long life, I have my struggles with health issues. Yet I am so lucky, as my mind and soul are still strong. I have told my story now, and I am surrounded and cared for by people who love me. I have nothing to fear.

If God ever had a plan for me, it was to be a mother. I am privileged and honored to have nurtured and raised such incredible individuals. They have contributed so much, not just to their families and communities, but to the world at large. Their own children continue in their footsteps.

Our actions create effects that ripple outward through time and distance, and so we must always do our best with the gifts we have. Sometimes we do not realize what we gave to the world until later. That realization is humbling and gratifying, when we understand how many lives we can touch, no matter where our journeys begin or end.

During my life, I have been known by many names.

Some were dismissive: Japon, or Bata—and yet these were the names of a child who survived unimaginable hardship. Diamond was the name given to me when Doming Apostol rescued me, and it was the name I could proudly write. Mama Diamond was the name given to me by my charges when I served as their nanny. Being called Mrs. Apostol had always felt strange to me, but it was an honor, since it was the name of the husband I loved. Being called Mama is a privilege I have always treasured. And now, many years later, to be called Grandma is another blessing.

So many names. But at last, I reclaimed the one given to me at birth and lived the rest of my life with certainty. I am, I always have been, Etsuko Miyagi.

# SOME BACKGROUND INFORMATION ON THE PHILIPPINES

## *The Archipelago*

In learning the story of Diamond, it is helpful for readers to understand more about the geography, history, and climate of the Philippines nation.

The Philippines consists of approximately seven-thousand-six-hundred islands. It is an island nation with a prime location, at just the right place on Earth to be coveted by all countries around it. Its shining position on the Pacific Ocean puts it within sailing distance of Japan, China, India, Southeast Asia, Vietnam, Laos, Cambodia, and Arabia.

This meant that, for centuries, people came to trade, live, and work in the Philippines from an incredible variety of places. And, of course, indigenous people had lived there already. Well over a hundred cultures were spread across the islands. These cultures and people mixed, forming beautiful customs, knowledge, and hybrid skills. The Philippines has incredible diversity– in its terrains, communities, races, production, and traditions.

### *The Philippines under U.S. Rule*

The Treaty of Paris, signed in 1898, concluded the Spanish-American War and resulted in Philippines' sovereignty being transferred from Spain to the United States, which acquired the archipelago for twenty-million dollars. Unfortunately, the indigenous Filipinos were not consulted or given the opportunity to voice their opinions in this matter.

Revolutionary leader Emilio Aguinaldo was president of the Philippines from 1898 to 1902, but neither the United States nor Spain recognized him, both of them claiming sovereignty over the archipelago. Despite this, Aguinaldo formally declared the independence of the Philippines from Spain on June 12, 1898, following the victory of American forces over the Spanish fleet in Manila Bay. He established the First Philippine Republic, also known as the Malolos Republic, and drafted a constitution that was ratified by a revolutionary assembly.

The United States, however, refused to recognize the legitimacy of the Malolos Republic and its constitution and began to occupy the Philippines. The resulting Philippine-American War lasted from 1899 to 1902 and was characterized by resistance from Filipino guerillas against American forces. Aguinaldo was eventually captured by American forces in March 1901 and compelled to pledge allegiance to the United States, but Filipino guerilla tactics persisted in resistance to

American domination until approximately 1906.

In an attempt to pacify the Filipino resistance, future U.S. President William Howard Taft implemented the "policy of attraction" during his tenure as governor-general of the Philippines. This approach aimed to grant Filipinos greater autonomy in exchange for their loyalty to the American colonial government. However, Taft did not intend to grant full independence to the Philippines, but sought to establish a favorable, long-term relationship between the two countries.

In 1902, President Theodore Roosevelt declared the end of the war and granted pardon to Filipinos who had engaged in attacks against the United States, with a few exceptions for serious crimes.

While in occupation, Americans built several military bases because the Philippines provided an excellent location to keep control of that part of the Pacific Ocean. In the following years, the Philippines was left to manage its own affairs, although the United States could intervene at any point it chose, and be quite dominating in the process, if its military stake was threatened.

In 1907 the Philippines held its first national assembly, while the Jones Law of 1916 proposed the eventual emancipation of Filipinos once they could prove their ability to manage their own governance. Despite the significance of this law, a clear timeline for independence was not specified. In 1935, the Philippines achieved the status of a self-governing commonwealth, yet it was not until July 4, 1946, after the disastrous events of World War II, that the nation was granted complete independence from the United States.

In 1962 President Diosdado Macapagal modified the official date of Philippine Independence Day from July 4 to June 12, to commemorate Aguinaldo's declaration in 1898. People continue to celebrate that day annually as a symbol of their country's hard-won national pride.

### *Japanese Migration to the Philippines*

Before World War II, many Japanese immigrated to the Philippines in search of opportunities and brighter futures. Many of these Japanese lived in Davao City, the most important city on the island of Mindanao. They worked hard for years while facing discrimination from the locals, who were determined to keep them at bay. But with unwavering perseverance, these brave men and women built their businesses over time. Some prospered as landowners, while others became successful businesspeople or merchants.

Things began to change drastically for these Japanese immigrants as World War II approached and tensions rose between Japan and the Philippines. Many immigrants were compelled to leave their homes and businesses to avoid severe repercussions, such as relocation or imprisonment by occupying forces. But despite the odds, some chose to stay behind and continue working.

The Japanese invaded the Philippines in 1941 for two reasons: the archipelago's location, making it a prime point of transportation for oil to Japan, and because of its status as an American colony. The dramatic violence of this invasion resulted in hundreds of thousands of innocent deaths on both sides of the conflict. Diamond's Japanese parents and her youngest sibling were among those numbers.

Fortunately, diplomacy was achieved between the two nations in 1956, and today Japan and the Philippines enjoy friendly economic and collaborative ties.

### *The Island of Mindanao*

Mindanao, the second-largest island of the Philippines archipelago, is also the southernmost island. It is separated from Luzon, the largest island (where the capital city of Manila lies) by a vast group of islands called the Visayas.

Magpet, located on Mindanao, is part of the Cotabato Province, where some Bagobo tribes live in the foothills around the great Mount Apo. Magpet is approximately eighty-one miles from Davao, a large and progressive city. The Davao area was a busy trading port for centuries, but Davao itself only officially became a city a few years before World War II.

The climate of Mindanao is tropical, and the temperatures remain moderate year-round, mostly hovering in the warm and humid range of eighty to ninety degrees Fahrenheit. There are wet and dry monsoon seasons. The wet seasons are during the summer, June to November. December through May comprises the dry season. June through November is considered "typhoon season," although typhoons occasionally occur at other times of the year. About twenty typhoons (or hurricanes, as they are known in the western hemisphere) come from the southeast every year to sweep across the Philippines.

The people of the Philippines are called Filipinos. There are over one-hundred-seventy dialects spoken throughout the region, but the country's official languages are Filipino and English. The country also acknowledges the regional languages as auxiliary official languages within their respective areas. In Magpet, the dominant dialects spoken are Cebuano and Bisaya.

Made in the USA
Monee, IL
31 August 2024

2882bb44-5829-4554-b308-47b7ccf90d15R01